CALIFORNIA'S CENTRAL COAST

THE ULTIMATE WINERY GUIDE

CALIFORNIA'S CENTRAL COAST

THE ULTIMATE WINERY GUIDE

FROM THE SANTA YNEZ VALLEY TO PASO ROBLES

by **Mira Advani Honeycutt**

photographs by **Kirk Irwin**

foreword by **Jim Clendenen**

CHRONICLE BOOKS
SAN FRANCISCO

DEDICATION

To my parents: my father, Gobind Singh Mansukhani, who gave me the writing gene, and my mother, Kiki, who gave me the taste gene.

MIRA

To my wife, Beverly, whose love, encouragement, and support have made my life and my work a real joy.

KIRK

Library of Congress Cataloging-in-Publication Data available.
ISBN-10: 0-8118-5167-2
ISBN-13: 978-0-8118-5167-1

Design by *Scott Thorpe*
Typeset in Whitman, Noble, and Serifa

Manufactured in Hong Kong

Distributed in Canada by Raincoast Books
9050 Shaughnessy Street
Vancouver, British Columbia V6P 6E5

10 9 8 7 6 5 4 3 2 1

Chronicle Books LLC
680 Second Street
San Francisco, California 94107
www.chroniclebooks.com

ACKNOWLEDGMENTS

My special thanks to the winemakers, vintners, farmers, chefs, and members of the tasting room staffs who made this book possible by sharing their time and their spirit. My sincere acknowledgment to Jodi Davis, Bridget Watson Payne, Jim Clendenen, Jim Fiolek of the Santa Barbara County Vintners' Association, Stacie Jacob of the Paso Robles Wine Country Alliance, Chris Taranto, Kaitlin Wallace, Fran Clow, Peter Cargasacchi, Christine Forsythe, Cindy Newkirk, Emma Thomas, Charles Yates, Vicki Carroll, Becky Gray, Gordon Bennett, Tom Fuller, Monty Sander, Elaine Mellis, Rick Segovia, and Wes Hagen. My heartfelt appreciation to my two daughters, Tasha and Rishika, and my brother, Gulab, for their love and support, and last but not least to my husband, Kirk Honeycutt, for his love, enthusiasm, and time devoted in assisting me with this book.

MIRA ADVANI HONEYCUTT

The beauty of the wine country directly reflects the love of the land and its produce expressed by those who till the soil, tend the vines, and harvest the grapes. I thank all of the vineyard workers, managers, and owners for providing me with such magnificent scenes to photograph and for graciously allowing me to be a guest in their vineyards.

KIRK IRWIN

Contents

Is the Central Coast destined to be a victim of the "always a bridesmaid, never a bride" syndrome? I wonder. It doesn't even qualify for the maid-of-honor title, because that is the perpetual position of Sonoma County. The Central Coast counties of Santa Barbara and San Luis Obispo have been repeatedly identified and simultaneously stigmatized as areas of great potential. This identification follows precisely the boom-and-bust cycles that have existed historically in the wine business, which closely echo the same cycles in the overall U.S. economy. Closer scrutiny may reveal a special set of circumstances that, until now, have hindered recognition of the area as a great grape-growing region.

The region's history in winemaking is quite short. The majority of the plantings in both counties date from the early 1970s. The Miller family, Louis Lucas, Sam Hale, the Firestones, the Flood family, the Bettencourts, Louis Marshall Ream, and Richard Sanford with Michael Benedict began developing vineyards in Santa Barbara County. In San Luis Obispo County, pioneers were the Niven family, the Goldmans, Dr. Stanley Hoffman, and Cliff Giacobine with Gary Eberle at Estrella River Winery. The vast majority of the vineyards were established to sell grapes to existing wineries on the North Coast. When those sales were unsuccessful, more and more vineyard owners started wineries or wine brands to get their produce to market.

Santa Barbara County emerged first, along with Edna Valley in southern San Luis Obispo County, whose cool climate and coastal influence has much more in common with Santa Barbara's growing regions than with the rest of San Luis Obispo County. Firestone, Zaca Mesa, Sanford & Benedict, and Santa Ynez Valley Winery (SYVW) hired talented newcomers and embarked on a path to bring attention to the area. Economic conditions in the late 1970s, the scale of operations, and the ambitions of some of the newcomers combined to launch the county to its next level of recognition. Firestone begat Austin Cellars; SYVW begat Brander; Zaca Mesa begat Au Bon Climat, Qupé, Ojai Vineyard, Byron, and Lane Tanner; Sanford & Benedict begat Sanford.

The energy of the new wineries during the 1980s resonated throughout the industry. With Edna Valley Vineyards partnering with Chalone, and the success of Santa Barbara County, it became clear that one of the great areas for cool-climate coastal viticulture was, oddly enough, way down south of San Francisco. The upshot of this recognition was that North Coast wineries soon snapped up approximately 75 percent of the county's planted vineyards. The large-scale wineries making these purchases might not have been the best vehicles to continue and consolidate the success of the Central Coast. By the mid-1990s, the area had lapsed back into unfulfilled potential.

During Santa Barbara County's ascension, the Paso Robles region was struggling. It did a terrific job with Cabernet Sauvignon, but the category was already well-represented, with Napa and Sonoma making great Cabernet. It is possible that the area lacked the same dynamic leadership early on that generated attention for Santa Barbara. But in the late 1980s Ken Volk and Gary Eberle, among others, garnered the accolades that Paso Robles needed. By the mid-1990s, Paso Robles was much like Santa

Barbara. Large vineyards sold grapes where they could, and large wineries struggled for identity while watching their bottle prices fall. Medium-sized wineries like Eberle, Wild Horse, and Peachy Canyon had success, but were not especially comfortable in the economic climate, as they were being squeezed by larger wineries from famous areas. The stage was set for the new arrivals, specialists in Syrah, Grenache, Zinfandel, and Cabernet Sauvignon, who would pioneer riper and bolder styles of wine and achieve bottle prices not seen before in the Paso Robles area. These high-profile wineries, including Linne Calodo, L'Aventure, Saxum, Tablas Creek, and Treana, established a foundation of quality and visibility that had previously been elusive.

Santa Barbara and southern San Luis Obispo County were ready to emerge again. In the mid- to late 1990s, Talley Vineyards, Alban, and Chamisal received great recognition. Another generation of winemakers, including Brewer-Clifton, Sea Smoke, Drew Family, and Fiddlehead, reintroduced the wine-consuming public and wine journalists to high-profile, high-quality Santa Barbara wine. The newer appellations of Arroyo Grande Valley in southern San Luis Obispo County and the Santa Rita Hills in coastal Santa Barbara County gave wine critics a reason to return to the area.

By the early 2000s economic forces had conspired to cause problems for the Central Coast: a perception of overplanting, a shrinking distribution chain, a proliferation of new labels, and a general malaise among wine producers. Sometimes fads take over; witness Chardonnay in the late 1970s and Merlot in the 1990s. For Santa Barbara County, the popularity of Alexander Payne's quirky paean to Pinot, the 2004 film *Sideways*, defined another reemergence. It's ironic that a wine movie can spark a wine fad that can relaunch a region. Thanks to the hard viticultural labor in the Central Coast during the last twenty years, the area has prepared well for the attention of the media, tourism, international markets, and wine consumers. Yes, the attention turned through serendipity, perhaps of a fad, a movie, or a moment, but the area's potential, largely fulfilled, will keep the momentum going forward. The unique Central Coast microclimate caused by the Pacific Ocean's moderating influence will continue to produce grapes of distinctive character. After that, it is up to the energetic, passionate, and creative winemakers to play their role.

I have been making wine in the area for almost thirty years, and you'll be seeing more of me.

JIM CLENDENEN
Au Bon Climat

12

From Burgundy to California, the monks did more than build religious monuments. They planted vineyards. Nowhere is this more evident than in California's Central Coast region. In fact, it was Father Junipero Serra who planted more than a thousand vines in 1797, at the historic Mission San Miguel Arcangel in Paso Robles.

The sun-drenched landscape of the Central Coast wine country is studded with eucalyptus and pine trees and centuries-old oaks bent with age. Acres of manicured vineyards hug country roads, interspersed with the occasional weathered barn. The region is steeped in California's early history, from the native Chumash Indians to the Franciscan monks and Spanish land-grant rancheros to the Yankee ranchers and other settlers. Suffused with this rich past, the wine trails I offer in this book at times follow the old stagecoach routes.

On this journey, you will visit wineries nestled on the slopes of the Santa Ynez Valley and Edna Valley, farms hidden away off Templeton's rural roads, and inns and art galleries in such alluring hamlets as Ballard and Los Olivos. You'll enter wine-tasting rooms sandwiched between Danish pastry shops in Solvang, and sample gourmet food and visit antiques shops in the historic town square of Paso (as locals refer to Paso Robles). You'll encounter old barns refurbished into charming tasting rooms and stagecoach stops reincarnated as quaint inns and restaurants. And you'll savor Santa Ynez and Los Alamos, towns that evoke a bygone era.

What's so special about the Central Coast wine region? In a word, it is *diversity*, in both climate and the winemakers drawn to the area. The varied microclimates support just about every grape, from Bordeaux and Burgundy to Rhône and Italian vari-etals. Pinot Noir dominates the western part of the Central Coast. Rhône varietals thrive in the mid-region's moderate climate, and Cabernet Sauvignon and Merlot in the far east. This diversity draws icon-oclastic winemakers, especially those in Paso who are conjuring blends of wine you will not experience elsewhere. Although Paso is known for blending Rhône and Bordeaux, when it comes to Pinot Noir, purists stay true to this delicate and often fickle grape.

The vast Central Coast wine region stretches from Santa Ynez Valley in the south and snakes all the way to lower San Francisco Bay in the north. It is framed on the west by the Pacific Ocean and on the east by the towering Sierra Madre Mountains and by Los Padres National Forest. This book concentrates on the southern and central part of the region, divid-ing it into two sections: Santa Barbara County and San Luis Obispo County. Narrowing the winemakers to just thirty was a challenge, and I encourage you to explore the Central Coast wine country on your own and discover your favorites.

SANTA BARBARA COUNTY

More than a hundred wineries are spread through-out the county in three appellations – Santa Ynez Valley, Santa Maria Valley, and Santa Rita Hills – and in Los Alamos Valley. Although not a designated American Viticultural Area (AVA), Los Alamos is the county's fourth most important growing area and its largest. As you drive along Highway 101 through Los Alamos, you'll see miles of vineyards owned by such large companies as Sutter Home, Beringer, and Kendall-Jackson.

The first post-Prohibition winery that revital-ized the region was not in one of the valleys but in downtown Santa Barbara, established by retailer Pierre Lafond in 1962. By the early 1970s, he was joined by Brooks Firestone, scion of Firestone Tire and Rubber, who established a facility bearing the

Firestone, and Fess Parker. Santa Maria Valley, the county's northernmost appellation, is home to the nine-hundred-acre Bien Nacido Vineyards. Fruit from this famed vineyard finds its way into more than one million bottles each year. Plantings start at the valley floor and sweep up to an elevation of eight hundred feet.

While both Santa Maria and Santa Ynez enjoy cool to warm temperatures, the Santa Rita Hills area is blessed with cool marine air, a condition that allows Pinot Noir to thrive. In this newest appellation, you'll find wineries along the parallel thoroughfares of Santa Rosa Road and Highway 246, stretching from Buellton to Lompoc. The Santa Rita Hills was pioneered by Richard Sanford when he planted Pinot Noir in the Sanford & Benedict Vineyard in the early 1970s. It wasn't until 2001 that the region received its AVA designation, credited largely to the efforts of Wes Hagen, viticulturist and winemaker at Clos Pepe Vineyards and Winery. Hagen sees this region as "a grand slam. We've got the fruit blessing from California, sun and acidity from the cool climate, and complexity from the high calcium soil." Besides the soil and climate, there's a third component that makes the entire county special, and that is *alma* (Spanish for "soul"). "The French call it *terroir*, we call it *alma*; our wines are imbued with that spirit," asserts Jim Fiolek, executive director of the Santa Barbara County Vintners' Association.

Not all of the county's wineries, however, are open to the public. A select group of winemakers creates limited quantities of handcrafted wines in such unromantic places as industrial warehouses and custom crush facilities. One cluster of individual production facilities, dubbed the Lompoc Ghetto, has evolved into a hotbed of winemaking. Kris Curran (winemaker for Seasmoke Vineyards) makes limited quantities of Syrah and Grenache Blanc under her Curran label. She is joined by such pedigreed names as Brewer-Clifton, Palmina, Longoria, Fiddlehead, and Stolpman. A few miles north at Santa Maria's Central Coast Wine Services, winemakers share the equipment in a 210,000-square-foot warehouse. Wines produced here include such labels as Lane Tanner, Arcadian, Dierberg, Cordon,

family name, and by Bill Mosby of Mosby Wines, the Bettencourt and Davidge families of Santa Ynez Valley Winery, and Richard Sanford of Sanford Winery. The opening of Zaca Mesa Winery in the mid-1970s drew emerging winemakers, such as Ken Brown, Daniel Gehrs, Rick Longoria, Lane Tanner, Bob Lindquist, Adam Tolmach, and Jim Clendenen, who went on to leave an indelible mark on Central Coast wines.

North of Santa Barbara lies the Santa Ynez Valley, a long east-west corridor with temperatures that are cool on the coast and progressively warmer inland. The valley has five small towns, Los Olivos, Buellton, Solvang, Santa Ynez, and Ballard, home to the majority of the region's wineries and tasting rooms. Vineyards range in elevation from two hundred feet near the Santa Ynez River to fifteen hundred feet in the San Rafael Mountains.

A scenic twenty-mile route through Foxen Canyon, a popular destination for bicyclists, links Santa Ynez Valley and Santa Maria Valley. Passing by rustic ranches, you'll find wineries such as Foxen, Koehler, Andrew Murray, Zaca Mesa, Curtis,

Kunin, J. Wilkes, Summerland, Steven Ross, Westerly, Ovene, Labyrinth, Costa de Oro, and Hitching Post. Although you can't visit this cooperative facility, you can sample the wines at tasting rooms and wine shops in Solvang and Los Olivos.

SAN LUIS OBISPO COUNTY

Arroyo Grande Valley and Edna Valley, two small appellations located in the county midway between Santa Maria Valley and Paso Robles, are home to more than twenty-five wineries. This corridor enjoys one of the longest growing seasons in the county, due to the cool Pacific breezes funneled through Los Osos Valley straight into the mouth of Edna Valley, which runs east-west for eight miles and is framed by the towering Santa Lucia Mountains. The regions of Edna Valley and Arroyo Grande Valley received their AVA designation in 1982 and encompass approximately thirty thousand acres. The approach to this area's wineries is through the historic town of Arroyo Grande, which leads to the expansive valley cradled by the towering Santa Lucia Mountains. Acres of vineyards sweep the valley floor where most of the wineries are located, some along Orcutt Road and others on Route 227, with a handful tucked along backcountry roads.

The more than a hundred wineries of Paso Robles are grouped into three distinct wine trails: off Highway 101, located on Highway 46 East, they are known as the Eastside Wineries, while the ones on Highway 46 West are referred to as the Westside Wineries. The third trail, on Paso's west side, is in Adelaida Hills, reached by scenic Adelaida Road. Winding around vineyards, oak groves, and walnut orchards and through the Santa Lucia Mountains, Adelaida Road leads to twelve wineries appropriately called the Far Out Wineries. Another group on the east side of Paso, known as the Back Road Wineries, are small family-owned wineries, each producing one thousand to five thousand cases annually.

Paso has come a long way since its first commercial winery, the Ascension Winery. Now known as York Mountain Winery, it was established in 1882 by Indiana rancher Andrew York. The family planted some of the area's earliest Zinfandel grapes, making Paso famous for this varietal. This is the only winery in the six-thousand-acre York Mountain appellation (designated an AVA in 1983), located between Paso Robles and Cambria.

Although Paso's wine philosophy was shaped in the 1970s by California wine-industry guru André Tchelistcheff, Dr. Stanley Hoffman is hailed as the area's godfather. The Beverly Hills cardiologist traded ten acres of his Ventura County land for twelve hundred acres in Paso. He was the first vintner to plant Cabernet Sauvignon and Pinot Noir (these vine cuttings came from Burgundy) on his Hoffman Mountain Ranch on the hillsides of Adelaida, on Paso's west side. In the mid-1970s, Hoffman's HMR Pinot Noir was entered in a blind tasting in France and beat out some prestigious Burgundian domaines. This international recognition put Paso on the map. Another trailblazer, Matt Garretson of Garretson Wine Company, championed the Rhône varietals and is regarded as the force behind Hospice du Rhône, the annual charity event held in May.

Something about Paso's Wild West history attracts renegade winemakers who create unusual proprietory blends, dubbed "Super Paso." This maverick spirit is apparent at the Zinfandel Summit, a seminar celebrating the region's heritage grape, held during the Zinfandel Festival in March. The twelve Far Out Wineries participate in the event, where you can learn about this Mediterranean grape and get a sense of Paso's spirited winemakers.

Besides savoring wine and cuisine, you can learn about Paso's agriculture on a tour at the Wine Yard with Cindy Newkirk (a third-generation farmer) in her rustic fifty-year-old Jeep, "Willy." The roller-coaster ride will take you along the steep contours of Steinbeck Vineyards, owned by her father, Howard Steinbeck.

As a longtime Los Angeles resident, I've enjoyed the close proximity to the Central Coast wine country. My love for this region's food and wine, and especially the vintners and farmers, continues to grow. And so will my future trips to explore new wineries. I encourage you to seek out your favorite wines and savor the bounty and spirit of the Central Coast. ⌃

Whether you're driving along the freeway or on back-country roads, you'll see citrus orchards and fields of broccoli, lettuce, squash, artichokes, and strawberries, along with roadside stands selling just-picked fruits, nuts, and vegetables. Both Santa Barbara County and San Luis Obispo County are known for their farms, many of them specializing in organic produce that is so highly regarded it winds up on the tables of some of southern California's toniest restaurants.

Some of these farmers traded their urban careers for life on a farm. Fondly known as the "tomato lady" for her two hundred varieties, Barbara Spencer of Windrose Farms was a studio musician in John Williams' orchestra until she decided to give up her cello for a shovel. She left Los Angeles for San Luis Obispo County in the early 1990s, purchased a fifty-acre farm in Paso, and serendipitously met her future husband, Bill Spencer, a former rancher. From a handful of tomato seedlings, the Spencers' farm has expanded to include fruit orchards with apple, nectarine, and peach trees, row crops, an herb garden, and a flock of sheep. To experience the Spencers' farm haven, you can attend the tomato tasting and buffet held in September or enjoy summer camping on the property.

After twenty-nine years as a homicide detective for the Los Angeles County sheriff's department, Dick Rogers wanted a radical change when he retired. On a camping trip to the Central Coast, Rogers and his wife, Kim, came across Highway 46 West and found their future home, Hollyhock Farms, in Paso. "I went from killing fields to tomato fields," he muses. Beginning in the mid-1990s, they started farming their thirty-acre ranch in Paso. Tomatoes, cantaloupes, a variety of onions and squashes, and flowers marked with a "U-Pick Flowers" sign fill the fields. A pen holds a herd of Jacob sheep, which Rogers raises to help preserve the rare breed. The farm's organic eggs with chocolate brown shells come from French Cuckoo Marans chickens. A farm-stay program allows visitors to experience the farm firsthand, or to soak in country tranquility in a one-bedroom cottage adjacent to the residence. The Hollyhock roadside stand outside the farm is open from June through October.

In nearly every tasting room you visit in Paso, you'll see bottles of Pasolivo olive oil, produced by Karen Guth at her 130-acre Willow Creek Olive Ranch on Paso's west side. A trip to Tuscany, which reminded Guth of the area around her hometown, planted a seed: since Paso has its share of vineyards, why not grow olive trees? "It was sort of the anti-grape for me," laughs Guth. She took olive propagation classes at UC Davis and planted an olive grove that now numbers more than nine thousand trees, predominantly Tuscan varieties along with Greek, Mission, and Manzanillo. A certified taster of olive oils, Guth explains that the three attributes of olives – fruitiness, bitterness, and pungency – should all be in balance in an extra-virgin oil. The pungency comes from polyphenol, a phytochemical that contributes to the oil's health benefits. A grassy aroma and a peppery taste in the throat determine an oil's freshness and high quality. Guth and her team press the olives within hours of picking. Only the first press is bottled as extra-virgin. The ranch is open to the public for tastings Friday through Sunday. If you happen to visit in November, you can see the oil pressing in progress.

Of the numerous farmers' markets, the Saturday-morning market in Templeton is one of the most popular. The stands display more than fresh produce: Ben's pork and sausage, Odette's hot Louisiana sauce, seventy varieties of roses from Eufloria Flowers, and hormone-free, grass-fed beef from Old Creek Ranch. At Pure and Simple Artisan Bakers, you can sample Sandra and Mike Diamond's rosemary focaccia topped

23

with three cheeses, potatoes, and arugula, a meal in itself. For their mouthwatering pastries, the Diamonds handpick the fruit from neighboring farms.

Driving along Paso's Highway 46 heading west, you'll come across Jack Creek Farms, a vast ranch filled with vintage farm implements, vegetables and flowers in summer, and decorative gourds, squashes, and pumpkins in fall. A rare variety grown here, the Cinderella pumpkin, gained its name because it was the inspiration for the fairy-tale's illustrator. Fifth-generation farmer Joy Barlogio believes that this variety was served at the Pilgrims' second Thanksgiving. "The seeds were scooped out, it was filled with cream, eggs, honey, and spices, the lid was put back, and the pumpkin was buried in the ashes." Once cooked, it was eaten like custard—an early version of pumpkin pie. You can easily spend the better part of a day on this farm, picking sunflowers, petting farm animals, and exploring the apple orchard and demonstration garden. Come Labor Day weekend, you can take part in the annual Threshing Bee, a field-to-table experi-

ence where you help turn standing grain into stone-ground flour, which is then made into bread by students from a local culinary academy.

If you're traveling along Adelaida Road to the Far Out Wineries, Mt. Olive Organic Farm is a good place to pick up freshly made sandwiches for a picnic. Owners Karen and Reiner Ng stock their farm store with an assortment of freshly baked breads, organic sprouts, dried fruits, nuts, olives, and Asian-style beef jerky. The Ng family might even give you a tour of their worm-casting farm.

A few miles south of Paso in the quiet town of Santa Margarita lies the famous Rinconada Dairy, known for handcrafted cheeses made from raw sheep's milk. Owner Christine Maguire founded the dairy in 1999 with eight East Friesian ewes and one ram sired by a national champion. Maguire is known for her Pozo Tomme (similar to pecorino), a pressed cheese aged for two months. Smooth and creamy Chaparral is made from blending milk from sheep and Nubian goats. The dairy is not open to the public, but the cheeses are available in local gourmet stores, and make a delectable addition to your picnic basket.

The abundant local produce and wine draw a pool of chefs attracted to the wine-country lifestyle. Rick Manson came to the Central Coast from his native Georgia. His restaurant, Chef Rick's, in Santa Maria, offers a menu best described as "Deep South meets Southwest." Manson came to visit his parents in Santa Maria Valley in the late 1980s, when not much was happening on the local dining scene. He met vintners Jim Clendenen of Au Bon Climat and Dick Doré of Foxen Vineyard, who encouraged him to open a restaurant. Manson started off catering before opening his restaurant in a former pie shop. Although located in an unfashionable strip mall, Chef Rick's is a popular hangout for local winemakers. Manson's creations are so multilayered that you'll experience a multitude of flavors and textures—crunchy, smoky, spicy, tangy, creamy—in a single entrée. A dish might come topped with crispy spinach, crunchy crawfish, or a thin onion crisp, or might rest on a bed of Cheddar grits or shrimp dirty rice alongside broccoli slaw or fried green tomatoes. "One good thing on top of another" is how Manson

describes his approach. This is food that stands up to big, bold Central Coast Syrahs, Zinfandels, and Rhône blends.

Iowa-born siblings Jeff and Matt Nichols were trained in Paris and worked at such tony restaurants as Spago and Trump's in Los Angeles. When the wine country beckoned, they headed north and in the mid-1990s opened their first Brothers restaurant in a Solvang bed-and-breakfast. Within a few years, they were ready to take over the historic Mattei's Tavern, a former nineteenth-century stagecoach stop in Los Olivos. Stepping inside the restaurant, you're immersed in the past: photographs of the Old West line the walls, and guest registers and menus from early years fill a glass case. The only modern touch is the open kitchen presided over by Matt and Jeff. The menu changes weekly, inspired by the season: sweet corn soup in summer and earthy potato and leek soup in fall. With steaks, veal chops, and classic roast chicken also emerging from the kitchen, this is home cooking served bistro style.

Another local hub, the Hitching Post, is known for its Santa Maria–style barbecue, dating back to Spanish rancheros who grilled over open fires of red oak. Few match the grilling skills of vintner/chef/restaurateur Frank Ostini, whose family established the first Hitching Post in Casmalia in 1952. At the Buellton location, you get a good view of the industrial-size grill in action as steaks, chicken, and ostrich meat are seared, smoked, and grilled to perfection. The iceberg lettuce salad and shrimp cocktail are throwbacks to the 1960s. The specialty is grilled artichokes, trucked in from nearby Castroville. On one occasion, Ostini recalls, some diners left the restaurant without eating, disappointed that artichokes were not on the menu. "After that, we've never run out of artichokes." With his winemaking partner Gray Hartley, Ostini produces a limited quantity of exceptional Pinot Noir under the Hitching Post label. Wine tasting is conducted at the restaurant's bar from 4–6PM, a time when most other tasting rooms are closed.

As the new owner of the Ballard Inn and Restaurant, Budi Kazali has taken the dining room to new heights, earning its reputation as the French Laundry of the Santa Ynez region. Although breakfast and afternoon appetizers are only for inn guests, dinners (served Wednesday through Sunday) and the wine-tasting bar (operating daily) are open to the public. Kazali's classic French cuisine has an Asian accent. He marries mango with foie gras and grilled quail with Thai spices. Prince Edward Island mussels float in a Chardonnay–kaffir lime broth, and pan-seared Maine scallops come cradled on a bed of risotto flavored with lemongrass.

If you happen to approach Santa Ynez over the San Marcos Pass, be sure to visit Cold Springs Tavern, a nineteenth-century stagecoach stop turned restaurant. You'll get a taste of the Old West as you dig into chef Moises Bernal's variations on chili made with venison, rabbit, beef, or chicken. The tavern is open for lunch and dinner and weekend breakfast. Live music keeps the place hopping on weekend evenings. On Sunday afternoons, Harley riders out for a cruise stop by.

When Bistro Laurent, Paso's first French restaurant, opened in 1997, it surprised the locals. "They thought we were nuts, but we proved them wrong," asserts Laurent Grangien. After cooking in France and Los Angeles, Grangien settled in Paso's emerging wine region, as it reminded him of Europe. At his bistro, the menu changes weekly, depending on what's in season. You might see saffron-laced bouillabaisse, rabbit compote, and fricassee of sweetbreads and mushrooms with truffle butter. Around the corner at Paris Restaurant, owners Claude and Chrystel Chazalon whip up French specialties such as Burgundy snails in garlic sauce, onion soup, and homemade duck foie gras.

Veteran restaurateur and winemaker Chris Cherry moved from San Diego to Paso in 1996 after hearing about the region from friends. But what really made an impact was an article by wine critic Robert Parker, Jr., who hailed Paso as an emerging viticultural region. This made Cherry aware of Paso's potential. He purchased an old cattleman's bar in Paso's historic square and refurbished it as Villa Creek. Cherry and his chef, Tom Fundaro, have created a menu that harks back to early California's Mexican and Spanish flavors. Signature dishes include

butternut squash enchiladas with vegetable succotash and adobe-brick chicken, so named because a brick weighs down the chicken as it cooks in the pan. Both Central Coast and international wines appear on the impressive wine list. Be sure to sample Cherry's Villa Creek wines, especially Mas de Maha, a deep, rich blend of Temperanillo, Grenache, and Mourvédre.

A small-town airport is an unlikely place for a restaurant, but Matthew Riley, chef/owner of Matthew's at the Airport, makes good use of the space. Between wrapping quails in grape leaves in the kitchen and greeting guests at the front door, Riley can be seen on the tarmac, smoking salmon covered with Pinot Noir vine cuttings.

Templeton's oldest commercial building–dating to the 1860s–houses McPhee's Grill. Chef/restaurateur Ian McPhee was unable to choose between accepting a football scholarship or entering an architecture program, so he settled on air-conditioning engineering, a far cry from cooking. McPhee's part-time restaurant jobs got him hooked on the business. The self-taught cook realized his calling when he made a successful Thanksgiving meal with the help of the *Better Homes and Gardens Cookbook*. After stints at various restaurants, McPhee opened Ian's in Cambria in 1983, where he served ten basic dishes that he'd perfected. His repertoire soon expanded to recipes culled from Chez Panisse and Martha Stewart cookbooks. Although his cookbook collection has expanded to more than two hundred titles, McPhee notes that the books serve as an inspiration, as he has the ability to look at a recipe and capture its essence. McPhee moved to Templeton and opened McPhee's Grill in the mid-1990s. The menu combines regional dishes that make the best of local produce and straightforward fare such as pastas, pizzas, and salads.

Around Paso's historic town square you'll find a number of gourmet stores and wine bars. A courtyard along a side street holds a cluster of stores. We Olive stocks everything olive-related, from tapenades to body products, and holds olive-oil tastings. You can sample wines by the glass at the Wine Attic and pick up picnic items here or at the adjoining Lucinda's Pantry. Across the street, Di Raimondo's offers Italian delights and a variety of pâtés and cheeses. Nearby Vinoteca, a wine bar, serves local and international wines by the glass. You can also order appetizers and small plates.

If at the end of your wine country sojourn you crave a simple pizza, swing by American Flatbread, which occupies a Victorian house in Los Alamos (open on weekends only). Prayer flags line the courtyard. Inside, a large brick oven shaped like a beehive dominates the dining area, and a bar serves a good selection of local handcrafted wines by the glass. But it's the wood-fired all-natural artisanal pizza topped with organic ingredients that draws the crowd. *⁄⁄*

GOURMET TO GO: Places to pick up salads, sandwiches, and picnic items

SANTA YNEZ VALLEY

El Rancho Market / Gourmet Deli
2886 Mission Drive
Solvang
805.688.4300

Los Olivos Grocery
2621 Highway 154
Los Olivos
805.688.5115

Panino
2900 Grand Avenue
Los Olivos
805.688.9304

New Frontiers Natural Marketplace
1984 Old Mission Drive
Solvang
805.693.1746

Pattibakes
240 East Highway 246, No. 109
Buellton
805.686.9582

The Chef's Touch
1555 Mission Drive
Solvang
805.686.1040

EDNA VALLEY

Fiala's Gourmet Deli
1653 Old Price Canyon Road
San Luis Obispo
805.543.1313

PASO ROBLES

Berry Hill Bistro
1114 Pine Street
805.238.3929

Dining with André
1032 Pine Street
805.227.4100

Di Raimondo's Italian Market & Cheese Store
822 Thirteenth Street
805.238.1268

Lucinda's Pantry
1307 Park Street
805.237.0220

Mt. Olive Organic Farm
3445 Adelaida Road
805.239.4257

Panolivo
1344 Park Street
805.239.3366

Wilmot Market
725 Thirteenth Street
805.227.0148

Wine Attic
1305 Park Street
805.227.4107

27

The Central Coast wine country evokes the spirit of the late 1800s, when stagecoaches carried passengers, and outlaws rode into town. Remains of the Old West linger on, but now in place of blacksmith shops and mercantile stores you find fine restaurants, boutiques, inns, and wine-tasting emporiums. However, most of these small towns maintain their historical antiquity. Downtown can still be two or three blocks long, and old-fashioned parades continue to delight the locals. So take time out to explore the nostalgic charm of these small towns, browse through an antiques shop, relax in a café, and take in the towns' leisurely pace.

SAN LUIS OBISPO COUNTY

Paso Robles

Noted for its healing hot springs, El Paso de Los Robles (Spanish for "Pass of the Oaks") was once part of a Mexican land grant. In 1857, Daniel and James Blackburn, along with Lazarus Godchaux, purchased the town from Don Petronilo Rios for eight thousand dollars. Some years later, the Blackburns were joined in partnership with Drury James, uncle of the notorious outlaw Jesse. A stagecoach line brought customers to the local sulfur springs.

With the arrival of the railroad in 1886, plans for expansion went into high gear, with an opera house, a train depot, stores, and banking services. The town drew international visitors, among them Polish pianist Ignacy Paderewski, who set up residence at the Hotel El Paso de Robles and planted Zinfandel vineyards nearby. Located in the town's historic square, the landmark Mission-style hotel was completed in 1891. Although it was declared to be "absolutely fireproof," a fire in 1940 destroyed all but the ballroom wing, which still sits on the northwest corner of the property. The hotel was reconstructed in 1942 as the Paso Robles Inn and is now a member of the Historic Hotels of America, a distinguished group of approximately two hundred hotels nationwide. The town square is ringed with gourmet restaurants, wine bars, and antiques stores. A farmers' market occupies the park on Saturday mornings.

Old Edna

The two-acre townsite of Old Edna lies within current-day Edna in the bucolic Edna Valley. In the early 1880s, when the narrow-gauge rail made it a rest stop for travelers, Edna was a bustling place with a butcher, a blacksmith, a general store, and a saloon and dance hall. In 1897, John Tognazzini purchased the townsite from Lynford Maxwell and constructed a building that served as a mercantile store with a dance hall above. Today, it houses Fiala's Gourmet Deli, which has a performing space and art gallery on the second floor. The twelve-hundred-square-foot Tognazzini farmhouse, built in 1908, is now Suite Edna, a bed-and-breakfast owned by Pattea Torrance, a San Luis Obispo resident. A few old cabins are scattered around the property, one containing historical memorabilia, another bearing a sign, "Edna School House," the home school for a handful of students including Paul and Edy Fiala's son. A third cabin, known as "the crib," was once used by call girls who entertained weary travelers. Over the past hundred years, the property has seen three owners, including the current Torrance family.

Arroyo Grande

A stroll along Branch Street, Arroyo Grande's main street, is a reminder of simpler times, when merchants addressed the locals by their first names and helped them carry packages out the door. The street honors Francis Z. Branch, who came here in 1832 on a bear-hunting expedition. Beguiled by the area's natural beauty, he purchased sixteen thousand acres and became a cattle rancher. Rail service arrived in 1881,

29

and soon Arroyo Grande was on its way to prosperity. Retaining its early charm, the quaint village has gift shops, cafés, vintage shops, and the oldest butcher shop in the county, the Arroyo Grande Meat and Butcher Shop, established in 1899. At Christmas, Arroyo Grande is transformed into a fairyland with lights. Festivals and parades take place year-round. The Saturday-morning farmers' market is renowned. The village's noted feature is the Swinging Bridge, originally built of rope in 1875 so residents could cross the Arroyo Grande Creek. The weather-damaged bridge was replaced several times and eventually reconstructed with cable in 1995. It is the only bridge of its kind in California.

Templeton

Although it looks like a place forgotten by time, Templeton became a boomtown in 1886 with the arrival of the Southern Pacific Railroad. It was initially to be called Crocker, after the vice-president of the railroad, but since his name already graced a town, it was named for Crocker's son, Templeton (becoming the only town along El Camino Real named for a person and not a saint). The great fire of 1897 destroyed most of the business district. It was restored, but not to its former glory. The oldest surviving structure now houses the popular eatery McPhee's Grill. Visible from the freeway is the tall Feed and Grain building dating back to 1913. Initially built as a car and tractor garage, it was converted to a grain mill in 1930. Now a bed-and-breakfast, Templeton's oldest house was built in 1886 by C. H. Phillips. It survived the fire as it was located farther away from downtown's Main Street.

Santa Ynez

From 1882 to 1901, Santa Ynez Valley was an important stagecoach route between Los Angeles and San Francisco. The town itself began to take form in 1882, when Bishop Francis Mora received congressional approval to build a development called College Ranch, an area granted to the Catholic church. Settlers could purchase farmland for six to fifteen dollars per acre. Since the bishop felt it was more desirable for farmers to live in town than on farms, he offered a free lot in town with the purchase of an additional fifteen-dollar lot. The new settlement around Mission Santa Ines was to be named Sagunto in honor of the bishop's hometown in Spain. But the settlement never materialized, and the new town was established as Santa Ynez. With the arrival of the Southern Pacific Railroad came a boom in the 1880s and 1890s. There were eleven saloons, three livery stables, a school, a feed store, and a millinery shop. The town's first weekly newspaper was launched in 1887.

Santa Ynez still has a nineteenth-century Western ambience. The annual Old Santa Ynez Days held in June celebrates the past with food, music, and reenactments of the Old West. Sagunto Street is lined with half a dozen Western stores bearing such names such as Outpost Trading Company, Back at the Ranch, Old Adobe Traders, and Pony Express. In addition to the Maverick Saloon, the three-block long business district is home to two Italian restaurants, Volare and Grappolo's; tasting rooms; a coffeehouse; the Victorian-style Santa Ynez Inn; and the adjacent Vineyard House, serving regional cuisine.

Los Olivos

Named after the olive groves in the area, Los Olivos was established in 1886 as the main stop for a stage line that ran from San Francisco to Santa Barbara over San Marcos Pass. The stagecoach stop was at the town's hub – the Central Hotel, built by Swiss immigrant Felix Mattei. To draw prospective tourists and land buyers, a development company erected the Los Olivos Hotel, an elegant three-story hostelry

completed in 1888. When the Los Olivos Hotel burned down two years later, the Central Hotel changed its name to Hotel Los Olivos and was later renamed Mattei's Tavern. It is now the Brothers Restaurant at Mattei's Tavern, a popular dining place for locals and visitors. The stagecoach met its demise in 1901, due to the coming of the Southern Pacific Railroad and early automobile travel. The narrow-gauge railroad, the Pacific Coast Railway, meant for short hauls, continued its run to Los Olivos until 1934. Instead of blacksmith shops and general stores, Los Olivos has eclectic home and garden shops, cafés, the swank Fess Parker Wine Country Inn, and tony art galleries. The town has gained such a reputation as an art colony that the Los Olivos Art Gallery Organization now sponsors three annual art events, in March, in August, and over Thanksgiving weekend. Tasting rooms, including Andrew Murray and Daniel Gehrs's flower-draped heather cottage, line the three-block-long Grand Avenue.

Los Alamos

In 1876, John Bell and Dr. J. B. Shaw bought a couple of ranches from two original Mexican land grants and set aside a half square mile from each to establish Los Alamos. Among the town's historic landmarks is

the Union Hotel, built in 1880, which offered a bath, whiskey, and a meal to weary travelers arriving by stagecoach. The old Pacific Coast Railway station now houses the Depot Mall, an antiques and collectibles shop, and an adjoining pub. Along Bell Street, you'll also find antiques shops, a biker bar, and various eateries. Café Quackenbush serves hearty salads and sandwiches, and Twin Oaks fires up its oak pit barbecue to grill quail and prime rib. Farther up the street, at American Flatbread, the region's winemakers gather to order organic pizzas and local wines.

Ballard

A peaceful, unhurried pace prevails in the minuscule town of Ballard. New Yorker George W. Lewis homesteaded land in the area where Ballard and Los Olivos are now located. Because he spent most of his time in Mexico, Lewis left the property in the hands of his friend and neighboring rancher William N. Ballard, who recognized the need for a stagecoach stop on a route started in 1861. From 1860 to 1880, the Ballard Station served as the valley's first rest stop, where horses would be changed and travelers could kick off their boots and spend the night. In 1888, ten years after Ballard died, Lewis established the town of

Ballard. Ballard School, dating to 1883, was the first schoolhouse built in the county. At the time, it was the only public building in the valley, so it was also used for church services, weddings, funerals, and Saturday-night dances. Now known as the Little Red School House, it's the oldest serviceable school building in Santa Barbara County. The heart of Ballard is the fifteen-room country-style Ballard Inn and Restaurant, complete with white picket fence and wraparound porch. The heat from an oversized fireplace welcomes guests to the intimate lobby and popular dining room. Furnished with wicker furniture and rocking chairs, the porch makes an ideal spot to appreciate the tranquility of Ballard. ◎◦

All winemakers share a single philosophy: great wine begins in the vineyard. Applying the philosophy, winemakers and grape growers work together throughout the season to ensure the quality of fruit delivered to the winery. After a harvest that begins in August and can last until early November, the wines rest in barrels and the vines enter dormancy. Here is a look at a year in the operation of a vineyard.

NOVEMBER–MARCH: *Dormancy & Pruning*

An important period for grapevines, dormancy is a time when the vines rest and store energy for the production of shoots, leaves, and fruit for the following season. Chilling temperatures–at times dipping to twenty degrees Fahrenheit–cause the vines to go dormant and lose their leaves, hardening for winter. The vines are pruned by cutting back the canes to a certain number of spurs and buds per spur (the number of spurs and buds determines the tons-per-acre yield). Other factors influencing yield include weather, vine nutrition, soil, and farming practices during the growing season.

MARCH–APRIL: *Budbreak, Cover Crops,*
& Weed Control

A rise in daily temperatures and lengthening daylight bring on budbreak. Awakening from dormancy, the grapevines burst with new growth. Canes and leaves appear and rapidly expand to form a canopy. Budbreak also signals the beginning of the battle against powdery mildew, which can be combated with applications of sulfur or other organic and nonorganic compounds.

Cover crops bloom, creating a healthy environment for beneficial insects. For example, California poppies, bell beans, and radishes attract insects. Crimson clover fixes nitrogen in the soil, and rye and barley help control erosion.

Control of weeds is important at this stage so they do not choke the vines or compete for soil nutrition or moisture. Organic farmers practice hoeing, a costly procedure that is worth the effort as it aerates the soil, allowing for better water penetration. Other growers use minimum amounts of herbicides.

MAY–JUNE: *Bloom & Fruit Set, Vine Care,*
& Irrigation Management

Bloom and fruit set have various stages. In the pre-bloom stage, tiny grape clusters that look like flowers emerge. When the flowers open up, self-pollination takes place. All factors necessary to pollinate the fruit are self-contained in a single vine. If this is successful, the grape begins to grow to pea size. Once pollinated, the grape grows rapidly, accumulating mass, the grape's seed, and pulp.

Meticulous care is required during these months. Suckering–removal of all shoots from the grapevine trunk below the first trellis wire–allows the plant's resources to feed the upper shoots and also gives the vineyard a uniform look. Shoot positioning is done once the canes reach about twenty-four

inches. The canes are manipulated by hand and tucked onto the trellis wires in a vertical position, so that all growth is directed upward for optimal exposure to sunlight.

The removal of leaves from around grape clusters is practiced in cool climates to allow maximum exposure to sunlight and to promote ripening of the fruit. Sunlight on the fruit tames the unpleasant vegetal flavors and promotes floral compounds and the grape's color, critical for wine. It also inhibits mildew growth. The timing of leaf removal is very critical and is done when the fruit has finished setting, before the grapes grow large enough to touch each other. In hot climates, where fruit ripens easily, shade is necessary so the grapes do not burn.

Vineyards vary greatly according to soil, climate, rainfall, and other conditions, so irrigation management is crucial. Too much water gives the grapes a vegetal quality, a negative bell-peppery taste, and too little inhibits canopy growth, resulting in the vine's inability to mature. Dry farming is practiced in regions with sufficient rainfall and where the soil maintains moisture throughout the growing season.

JULY–AUGUST: *Verasion & Pest Control*

At the verasion stage, the grapes begin to soften and accumulate sugar, and their acidity lessens. Red wine grapes, green when they are young, begin to turn red.

Pest control plays a vital role in fruit quality and quantity. In the Central Coast, flocks of starlings and red-winged blackbirds start feeding on the grapes as harvest season approaches. Falcons, shotgun blasts, scarecrows, and flashy tapes are used to deter the birds. The only foolproof method of protecting the grapes is to cover the entire vine with netting, draping it eight feet over each side of the vine row. The netting also discourages squirrels and deer.

AUGUST–NOVEMBER: *Field Testing & Harvest*

Testing the sugar content of the fruit, done with a refractometer, indicates the readiness for harvest. The grapes need to be picked when they have a perfect balance of sugar and acid levels. Wait too long, and the grapes get too sweet and lose acidity, resulting in wine that is not food-friendly. Individual berries or whole clusters may be tested. To determine which clusters to test, a vintner might choose an odd number – say, five – and walk five rows in a given vineyard, go to the fifth plant, and then pick the fifth cluster on the vine. The procedure continues until

enough clusters are gathered for a random field sample, which is preferable to selecting only mature berries or clusters, an inaccurate field sample. The grapes are measured for sugar content and pH level (a scientific measurement to test the grape's acidity) in the vineyard or at the winery's laboratory.

Harvest is done by hand or mechanically. Hand-picking starts before sunrise. The clusters are cut off the vine and placed in small buckets that are transferred to half-ton bins pulled by a tractor through the fields. A mechanical harvester shakes the vines, dislodging the ripe fruit, which falls into conveyors that deposit the fruit in large bins. The fruit must be delivered cool to the winery, to keep the volatile acidity out of the whites and to prevent the reds from starting to ferment. Once the fruit is delivered to the crush pad, the winemaking process begins.

33

Winery Tours

WINERIES BY CENTRAL COAST REGION

SANTA BARBARA COUNTY

Santa Ynez Valley / Santa Maria Valley

Buellton / Solvang
Buttonwood Farm Winery & Vineyard
Lafond Winery & Vineyards
Rideau Vineyard
Rusack Vineyards

Foxen Canyon / Santa Maria
Cambria Estate Vineyard & Winery
Foxen Vineyard

Foxen Canyon / Los Olivos
Beckmen Vineyards
Fess Parker Winery & Vineyard

Lompoc
Babcock Winery & Vineyards
Melville Vineyards & Winery

Santa Ynez
Au Bon Climat/Cold Heaven Cellars
Gainey Vineyard
Sunstone Vineyards & Winery

SAN LUIS OBISPO COUNTY

Arroyo Grande Valley / Edna Valley

Arroyo Grande
Laetitia Vineyard & Winery
Talley Vineyards

Edna Valley
Baileyana Winery

Paso Robles

Highway 46 West / Far Out Wineries
Adelaida Cellars
Carmody McKnight Estate Wines
Justin Vineyards & Winery
Tablas Creek Vineyard

Highway 46 West / Templeton
Castoro Cellars
L'Aventure Winery
Summerwood Winery
Windward Vineyard

Highway 46 East / Paso Robles
Bianchi
Clautiere Vineyard
Eberle Winery
EOS Estate Winery
Martin & Weyrich Winery
Robert Hall Winery

WINERIES BY IDEAL VISITING SEASONS

Spring
Baileyana Winery
Beckmen Vineyards
Buttonwood Farm Winery & Vineyard
Castoro Cellars
Laetitia Vineyard & Winery
Summerwood Winery
Windward Vineyard

Summer
Buttonwood Farm Winery & Vineyard
Clautiere Vineyard
Fess Parker Winery & Vineyard
Justin Vineyards & Winery
Martin & Weyrich Winery
Rusack Vineyards

Autumn
Cambria Estate Vineyard & Winery
Eberle Winery
EOS Estate Winery
Laetitia Vineyard & Winery
Lafond Winery & Vineyards
Melville Vineyards & Winery
Robert Hall Winery
Talley Vineyards

Winter
Baileyana Winery
Fess Parker Winery & Vineyard
Rideau Vineyard
Rusack Vineyards
Sunstone Vineyards & Winery

Best Picnic Settings
Baileyana Winery
Beckmen Vineyards
Bianchi
Buttonwood Farm Winery & Vineyard
Cambria Estate Vineyard & Winery
Carmody McKnight Estate Wines
Castoro Cellars
Clautiere Vineyard
Gainey Vineyard
Eberle Winery
EOS Estate Winery
Fess Parker Winery & Vineyard
Justin Vineyards & Winery
Laetitia Vineyard & Winery
Martin & Weyrich Winery
Melville Vineyards & Winery
Rideau Vineyard
Robert Hall Winery
Rusack Vineyards
Summerwood Winery
Sunstone Vineyard & Winery
Talley Vineyards
Windward Vineyard

Caves
Eberle Winery
Robert Hall Winery
Sunstone Vineyard & Winery

Concerts / Theatrical Events
Adelaida Cellars
Bianchi
Carmody McKnight Estate Wines
Castoro Cellars
Clautiere Vineyard
Fess Parker Winery & Vineyard
Gainey Vineyard
Rideau Vineyard
Robert Hall Winery
Summerwood Winery

Elaborate Tasting Rooms
Au Bon Climat
Baileyana Winery
Bianchi
Cambria Estate Vineyard & Winery
Castoro Cellars
Clautiere Vineyard
Eberle Winery
EOS Estate Winery
Fess Parker Winery & Vineyard
Justin Vineyards & Winery
Lafond Winery & Vineyards
Martin & Weyrich Winery
Robert Hall Winery
Rideau Vineyard
Summerwood Winery
Sunstone Vineyards & Winery
Talley Vineyards

Gardens
Beckmen Vineyards
Buttonwood Farm Winery & Vineyard
Carmody McKnight Estate Wines
Castoro Cellars
Clautiere Vineyard
Fess Parker Winery & Vineyard
Gainey Vineyard
Justin Vineyards & Winery
Rideau Vineyard
Robert Hall Winery
Summerwood Winery
Sunstone Vineyard & Winery

Historical Interest
Baileyana Winery
Carmody McKnight Estate Wines
Foxen Vineyard
Rideau Vineyard
Talley Vineyards

Lunch and / or Picnic Provisions
Bianchi
Cambria Estate Vineyard & Winery
Castoro Cellars
EOS Estate Winery
Fess Parker Winery & Vineyard
Justin Vineyards & Winery
Martin & Weyrich Winery
Rideau Vineyard
Robert Hall Winery
Rusack Vineyards

Notable Educational, Food, and Wine Programs
Adelaida Cellars
Eberle Winery
Gainey Vineyard
Justin Vineyards & Winery
Rideau Vineyard
Robert Hall Winery
Summerwood Winery
Sunstone Vineyard & Winery
Tablas Creek Vineyard

Outstanding Design / Architecture
Bianchi
Clautiere Vineyard
EOS Estate Winery
Justin Vineyards & Winery
Martin & Weyrich Winery
Melville Winery
Robert Hall Winery
Sunstone Vineyard & Winery

Outstanding Panoramas
Babcock Winery & Vineyards
Baileyana Winery
Bianchi
Cambria Estate Vineyard & Winery
Castoro Cellars
Eberle Winery
Laetitia Vineyard & Winery
Robert Hall Winery
Talley Vineyards

Outstanding Tours
Eberle Winery
EOS Estate Winery
Gainey Vineyard
Justin Vineyards & Winery
Robert Hall Winery
Summerwood Winery
Tablas Creek Vineyard

Vineyard Visits
Adelaida Cellars (by appointment only)
Gainey Vineyard
Laetitia Vineyard & Winery

Wedding / Event Facilities
Carmody McKnight Estate Wines
Castoro Cellars
Eberle Winery
Fess Parker Winery & Vineyard
Gainey Vineyard
Martin & Weyrich Winery
Rideau Vineyard
Robert Hall Winery

Triangle Tours

Although many wineries are separated by only a ten- to fifteen-minute drive, the regions are large and spread out. The Foxen Canyon Trail in Santa Barbara County, for example, lined with a number of wineries, is twenty miles long and winding. And weekend traffic might cause travel-time delays between the towns of Santa Ynez, Buellton, Solvang, and Los Olivos. The Paso Robles wineries are in three areas—along Highway 46 East, Highway 46 West, and Adelaida Road. I suggest you visit no more than two wineries a day and be sure to leave time to take in the region's scenic beauty and historical interests. There are also farmers' markets to explore, antiques shops to browse, and cafés and restaurants to enjoy a meal.

Many tasting rooms have adjacent vineyards, so you'll want to check if it's permissible to explore the outdoors. There's nothing more delightful than a walk in the vineyards. Some wineries give tours, while others offer only tastings. Ask for a tour of the winery if it is adjacent to the tasting room. Except during harvest time, winemakers who are not too busy are usually happy to oblige.

For the wine tastings and tours below, the wineries are grouped according to area and are accompanied by listings of nearby restaurants for lunch and places to pick up picnic fare.

SANTA YNEZ VALLEY / SANTA MARIA VALLEY

Santa Ynez

Tasting at Au Bon Climat tasting room in Santa Ynez, lunch at Vineyard House restaurant next door, explore adjacent Victorian shops and Santa Ynez Historical Museum, and stop at Artiste tasting room and art studio.

Tour and tasting at Gainey Vineyard, pick up lunch at El Rancho Market, picnic and tasting at Sunstone Vineyard & Winery.

Buellton / Solvang / Los Olivos

Pick up lunch at Panino Cafe in Los Olivos, picnic and tasting at Rideau Vineyard, return to Los Olivos and visit art galleries, garden shops, and tasting rooms. Popular tasting rooms include Andrew Murray, Rick Longoria, Epiphany, the heather cottage of Daniel Gehrs, and the Los Olivos Tasting Room and Wine Store.

Pick up lunch at Los Olivos Grocery on Highway 154, picnic and tasting at Beckmen Vineyard, visit Mission Santa Inez.

Tasting at Lafond Winery & Vineyards in Lompoc, pick up lunch at Chef's Touch in Solvang, picnic and tasting at Buttonwood Farm Winery & Vineyard.

Visit Ostrich Farm, pick up lunch at New Frontiers Natural Marketplace, picnic and tasting at Rusack Vineyard, visit tasting rooms in Solvang and explore the town.

Lompoc

Pick up lunch at El Rancho Market in Solvang, tasting at Babcock Winery & Vineyard, picnic and tasting at Melville Vineyards and Winery.

Foxen Canyon Trail

Pick up lunch in Los Olivos; tour, tasting, and picnic at Fess Parker Winery & Vineyard; tasting at Foxen Vineyard; tasting at Cambria.

ARROYO GRANDE / EDNA VALLEY

Tasting at Laetitia Vineyard & Winery, pick up lunch at Fiala's Gourmet Café in Old Edna along Route 227, tasting and picnic at Baileyana Winery, tasting at Talley Vineyards.

PASO ROBLES / TEMPLETON

Far Out Wineries

Pick up lunch at Mt. Olive Company (open Thursday–Sunday), tasting at Adelaida Cellars, tasting and picnic at Carmody McKnight Estate Wines.

Tour and tasting at Tablas Creek Vineyard, tour and tasting at Justin Winery, lunch at winery's Deborah's Room restaurant (open Friday–Sunday).

Highway 46 West / Templeton

Pick up lunch at Main Street Market & Deli in Templeton, tasting at Summerwood Winery, tasting and picnic at Castoro Cellars.

Tasting at Windward Vineyard, lunch at McPhee's Grill on Main Street, tasting at L'Aventure Winery.

Highway 46 East / Paso Robles

Explore town of Paso Robles, pick up a picnic basket at Di Raimondo's Cheese Shop or Lucinda's Pantry, tasting and picnic at Martin & Weyrich Winery, tour and tasting at Eberle Winery.

Tour and tasting at Robert Hall Winery, lunch at Villa Creek in Paso Robles town square, tasting at Clautiere Vineyard.

Pick up lunch at Wilmot Market in Paso Robles, tasting and picnic at Bianchi, tour and tasting at EOS Estate Winery.

The Wineries

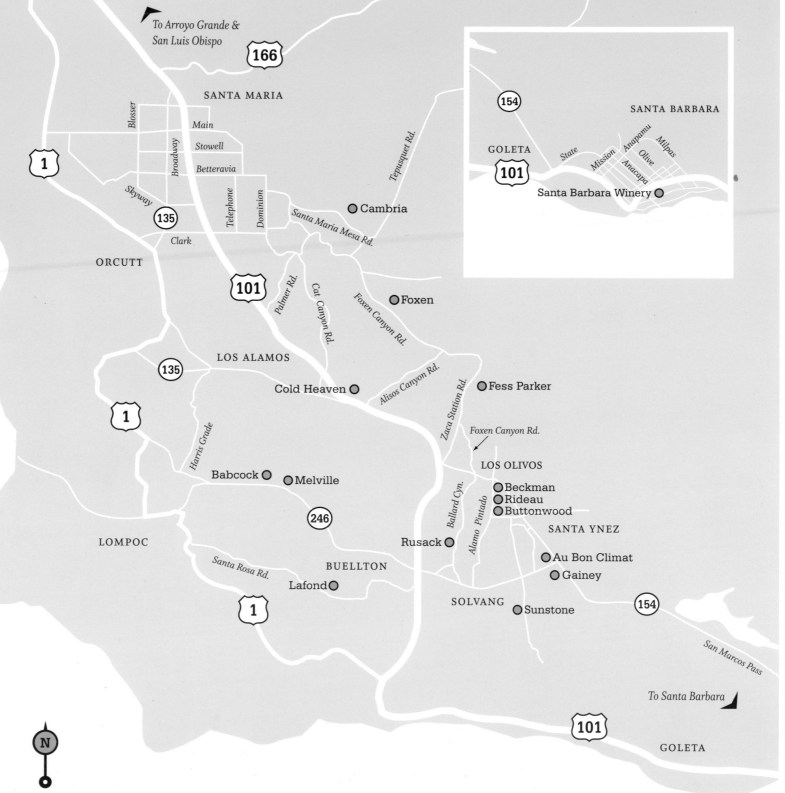

To Arroyo Grande &
San Luis Obispo

166

SANTA MARIA

Blosser

Main

Stowell

Broadway

Betteravia

1

Skyway

Telephone

Dominion

135

Clark

ORCUTT

Tepusquet Rd.

Santa Maria Mesa Rd.

◯ Cambria

GOLETA

154

SANTA BARBARA

State

Mission

Anapamu

Olive

Milpas

101

Anacapa

Santa Barbara Winery ◯

101

Palmer Rd.

Cat Canyon Rd.

Foxen Canyon Rd.

◯ Foxen

135

LOS ALAMOS

1

Harris Grade

Cold Heaven ◯

Alisos Canyon Rd.

Zaca Station Rd.

● Fess Parker

Foxen Canyon Rd.

LOS OLIVOS

Babcock ◯ ◯ Melville

Ballard Cyn.

● Beckman
● Rideau
● Buttonwood

SANTA YNEZ

246

Alamo Pintado

LOMPOC

Santa Rosa Rd.

BUELLTON

Rusack ●

● Au Bon Climat

● Gainey

Lafond ◯

SOLVANG

● Sunstone

154

1

San Marcos Pass

To Santa Barbara

101

GOLETA

N

PACIFIC OCEAN

Santa Ynez Valley
& Santa Maria Valley

THE WINERIES

Au Bon Climat / Cold Heaven Cellars

Babcock Winery & Vineyard

Beckmen Vineyards

Buttonwood Farm Winery & Vineyard

Cambria Estate Vineyard & Winery

Fess Parker Winery & Vineyard

Foxen Vineyard

Gainey Vineyard

Lafond Winery & Vineyards /
  Santa Barbara Winery

Melville Vineyards & Winery

Rideau Vineyard

Rusack Vineyards

Sunstone Vineyards & Winery

Au Bon Climat
Cold Heaven Cellars

OWNERS / WINEMAKERS: JIM & MORGAN CLENDENEN
OWNER / WINEMAKER: MORGAN CLENDENEN

When you read the label of any Au Bon Climat wine, you will see in small print the name of Jim Clendenen, followed by "Mind Behind." Not only is he the mind behind his famous wines, Clendenen has been a major force behind Central Coast wines.

Thanks to his larger-than-life personality and tireless marketing efforts, the proprietor and winemaker of Au Bon Climat (popularly known as ABC) has firmly established his wines and the Central Coast region on the international wine map. Au Bon Climat

Chardonnays and Pinot Noirs share space with the best of Bordeaux and Burgundy in the cellars of some of the finest restaurants in Europe.

Clendenen graduated from the University of California at Santa Barbara with high honors in pre-law. But a junior year abroad in 1974, when he found his true calling, derailed him from a law career. Three years later, he went back to France and spent time apprenticing in Burgundy's Chassagne Montrachet region. So struck was Clendenen by the hands-on Burgundian approach to winemaking that he was motivated to launch his own winery modeled after the small domaines of Burgundy. Returning to Santa Ynez Valley, he worked as assistant winemaker at Zaca Mesa Winery, long a training ground for the region's noted winemakers. In 1982, Clendenen with his then-partner Adam Tolmach (now the owner of Ojai Vineyards) established Au Bon Climat (meaning "a well-exposed vineyard") in a small dairy barn in Los Alamos. "We would start at six in the morning and pick the grapes. We pressed whole clusters, topped our barrels once a week, did everything by ourselves," recalls Clendenen of the early years when annual production was eighteen hundred cases. Even though production is now 100,000 cases a year (including all the labels made in the ABC warehouse), Clendenen continues to prefer the personal touch. "There's been a change in scale, not methodology," he says. "The style of wine has been consistent, and that's the secret to our success."

By 1986, Clendenen and Tolmach were joined by partners, including Bob Lindquist and Doug Margerum. The team established a second label, Vita Nova, also made in the dairy barn. As production grew, the group moved to a warehouse in Santa Maria. In 1989, they made the leap to the current warehouse in the foothills of Bien Nacido Vineyards. The original five-thousand-square-foot warehouse has expanded to a thirty-thousand-square-foot cavernous facility, with more footage planned for the future.

Clendenen describes his family of wines–including Au Bon Climat, Ici/La-Bas, Vita Nova, and Il Podere de Olivos – as enduring, food friendly, and multi-dimensional. His winemaking philosophy is all about that perfect balance between alcohol and acidity to produce a wine that will enhance a meal. He is not a proponent of high-alcohol wines: "They don't go well with food and conviviality. We want our wines to be energizing and stimulating and not the kind where you fall asleep at the dinner table," he says.

Some of the fruit for Clendenen's portfolio of wines is sourced from Bien Nacido Vineyards, where he has long-term contracts for sixty acres planted especially for him. Fruit for Pinot Noir, Viognier, and Chardonnay comes from Le Bon Climat, a one-hundred-acre vineyard he purchased in 1998 in Santa Maria Valley's minuscule town of Sisquoc (population two hundred). "I may be the town's mayor one day," laughs Clendenen.

Au Bon Climat is not open to the public throughout the year but is accessible at two open-house events, during the Santa Barbara County Vintners' Festival in April and the Harvest Festival in October. Large numbers of ABC aficionados come to the renowned Sunday lunches and wine tastings. As a local chef grills outdoors, Clendenen can be seen towering over a large pot, simmering a stew laden with spices and a good dose of wine. So popular are these events that at the October 2005 lunch, there was a shortage of plastic forks. Clendenen drove to the nearest store and returned in thirty minutes with supplies. If you're fortunate enough to attend one of these open houses, you'll sample a dozen or so varieties of Au Bon Climat wines, as well as tasting other handcrafted wines made by people who work under the ABC roof: Bob Lindquist's Qupé, Morgan Clendenen's Cold Heaven

AU BON CLIMAT TASTING ROOM: Santa Ynez Inn Wine Cellar // 3631 Sagunto Street, Santa Ynez, CA 93460

T 805.688.8688
F 805.686.4294
E syicellar@aol.com

www.santaynezwinecellar.com

ACCESS
From Highway 101, take Highway 154 exit and go 24 miles to Highway 246. Turn left and drive 1.2 miles to Meadowville Road and make a right. Then turn left on Sagunto Street. Tasting room is behind Vineyard House restaurant.

Hours for visits and tastings:
10AM – 4PM, Thursday – Monday.

Wheelchair access.

TASTINGS & TOURS
Charge for tasting: $10 for seven wines, three each of red and white, plus dessert wine. Includes glass.

No tours.

Typical wines offered: Chardonnay, Pinot Noir, and Italian varietals.

Wine-related items for sale.

PICNICS & PROGRAMS
Picnic area open to public. No picnic ingredients sold in the tasting room. Adjacent Vineyard House open for lunch and dinner daily.

Special events: Special gourmet dinners held at the Santa Ynez Inn featuring Au Bon Climat wines, and twice-annual open-house events at the winery in April and October. Check website for event calendar.

Cellars, Louisa Lindquist's Verdad, and Makor, produced by Jim Adelman, ABC's general manager.

But don't fret if you miss the ABC open houses. The wines can be sampled in the Au Bon Climat tasting room in Santa Ynez, housed inside the Coach House Antiques and Gifts shop and run by Christine and Doug Ziegler (owners of the adjacent Santa Ynez Inn). While Christine runs the antiques shop, Doug manages the tasting counter, pouring ABC's internationally recognized Chardonnays and prized Pinot Noirs from vineyards such as Bien Nacido, Sanford & Benedict, Talley's Rosemary's Vineyard, and Le Bon Climat Family Vineyard. You'll also get a taste of Italian varietals, such as Barbera and Nebbiolo.

While Clendenen's maverick nature has earned him the moniker of "Wild Man Jim," his wife, Morgan Clendenen, is the region's "Queen of Viognier." Morgan specializes in this varietal, making her Viognier austere and minerally tinged under her Cold Heaven Cellars label. She also makes a small amount of Syrah and Pinot Noir, totaling an annual production of one thousand to fifteen hundred cases. While producing Viognier is a secondary option for most winemakers, Morgan makes this fragrant grape her prime focus. As part of this focus, she has embarked on a Franco-American collaboration with winemaker Yves Cuilleron. What started off as a fun project when Morgan took her Viognier samples for blending to France has evolved into the Domaines des Deux Mondes label. A limited quantity of some two hundred cases is produced annually, with 50 percent of Morgan's Viognier from Santa Maria Valley and Santa Rita Hills blended with 50 percent of Cuilleron's Condrieu (Viognier) produced in the northern Rhône region. "It's a new experimentation for Yves, but he's getting a lot of flak in France for collaborating with a Santa Barbara County winemaker," muses Morgan. To sample Cold Heaven Cellars' lean and fresh Viognier, you'll have to visit Morgan's tasting room in Los Alamos. ⋏

COLD HEAVEN CELLARS TASTING ROOM: Heaven and Earth // 448B Bell Street, Los Alamos, CA 92440

T 805.344.3640
F 805.344.3614
E information@coldheavencellars.com

www.coldheavencellars.com

ACCESS
From Highway 101, take Los Alamos exit. At stop sign, turn right on Bell Street and go .5 mile. Tasting room is on right.

Hours for visits and tastings:
11AM–5PM, Friday–Sunday
or by appointment.

TASTINGS & TOURS
Charge for tasting: $10.

No tours.

Typical wines offered: Viognier, Syrah, Pinot Noir, and Clendenen Family Vineyard wines, including Chardonnay, Petit Verdot, Nebbiolo, and Barham-Mendelson Pinot Noir from Sonoma County.

Wine-related items for sale.

PICNICS & PROGRAMS
Picnic area not open to public. Quackenbush Café located next door.

Special events: Annual Foxen Canyon Wine Trail event. Check website for calendar.

Wine club.

Since beginning to make wine in 1984, Bryan Babcock has been on a mission to pinpoint the sections of soil within his vineyards that will give his wines their most distinctive qualities. He is a purist when it comes to *terroir,* the French word for a specific site whose climate and soil give the grapes their individual character.

Ask hundreds of French winemakers about *terroir,* and you will get hundreds of different viewpoints. For Babcock, it's simply an environmental signature. Although geography, climate, and farming techniques play an important role in determining the qualities of the grape, soil is the most critical. As Babcock notes, the different soils within any vineyard give the wine its individuality. For this reason, his line of Terroir Exclusives, a limited production of some two hundred cases, reflects the influence of each grape's respective *terroir.*

And how does Babcock determine which part of the vineyard is worthy of the *terroir* exclusive? After two decades' experience, he feels confident about defining the specific parts of his vineyards that deserve the appointed label on the bottles. "These are not just names of vineyards. These are profound, provocative, and distinctive wines that reflect a strong influence of the soil," asserts Babcock. Although the wines are primarily designed for the Terroir Exclusives wine clubs, those not sold after the first month are available in the tasting room. Depending on availability, some of these prized wines appear on the wine lists of high-profile restaurants.

The view from Babcock's hilltop winery is spectacular. From the parking lot, you see Chardonnay vineyards and, on either side, Pinot Gris vineyards he dubs "naughty little hillsides." This parcel of land has been a challenge for the winemaker: "Tractors slip, and shallow soil and wind make it difficult to farm, but it produces a very good Pinot Gris." Unlike a typical Pinot Gris, with its notes of high-tone fruit, this one is creamier, with more texture and a steely, mineral quality of a white Burgundy. Within the estate vineyards, the *terroir*-specific Chardonnay and Sauvignon Blanc come from Top Cream Vineyard behind the winery, a Syrah from Nook and Cranny Vineyard, and a Pinot Noir from the hillside Ocean's Ghost Vineyard. With seventy-five acres planted to Chardonnay, Sauvignon Blanc, Pinot Gris, Pinot Noir, and Syrah, the annual production comes to about twenty thousand cases.

Besides making wine from estate fruit, Babcock purchases fruit from special vineyards and seeks out the *terroir* within those vineyards. There is a Frying Pan Syrah (named after the vineyard's shape) from Alisos Vineyard, and a Cabernet Sauvignon called The Loin from Estelle Vineyard. The inky Radical Syrah comes from a two-acre chalky limestone parcel perched on a precipitously steep section of Hearthstone Vineyards in Paso Robles.

Bryan's parents, Mona and Walt Babcock, purchased the winery's 110-acre property in 1978, when the wine region was still in its embryonic stage. The couple wanted a retreat from Walt's dental practice and their two South Bay restaurants. By 1980 they had planted a twenty-five-acre vineyard, and within three years a number of local wineries were purchasing Babcock fruit. When Bryan graduated from Occidental College in southern California with a degree in biology and chemistry and then from the University of California at Davis with a master's in food sciences, they decided to start making their own wines with their first harvest in 1984.

Babcock's winery and tasting room are located in the Santa Rita Hills appellation and share the same driveway with Melville Winery. Don't let the plain interior of the tasting room fool you. Besides the lineup of Terroir Exclusives, you will taste a rich Rita's Earth Cuvée Chardonnay from Santa Rita Hills and a supple Tri Counties Cuvée Pinot Noir with fruit blended from Santa Barbara, Monterey, and Sonoma Counties. Best of all is the winery's flagship reserve wine: a deep, rich Bordeaux-style blend named Fathom.

The name Babcock selected for the wine refers to the problems he experienced making it. The blend was initially dominated by Cabernet Franc, but in the early to mid-1990s the Cabernet Franc fruit mysteriously went into decline. "The fruit didn't develop, and it got a severe virus," Babcock recalls. He then chose Merlot from vineyards such as Westerley and Vogelzang as the blend's backbone, along with Cabernet Sauvignon from Vogelzang. The Cabernet Sauvignon was so intense that Babcock proceeded to use this varietal as the key component. Given the travails, Fathom seemed the appropriate name. Future bottlings will continue to be Cabernet Sauvignon, with Cabernet Franc taking a supporting role. Babcock also produces a single varietal Cabernet Sauvignon from another of his favorite properties, the two parts of Estelle Vineyard, named Nucleus and Loin. The fruit will be used in future Fathom blends.

Babcock does not offer winery tours but will accommodate visitors with special requests, staff's schedules permitting. When tasting these *terroir*-appointed wines, see if you can identify the differences between the wines and ask your server the story behind each name. It will make your tasting experience all the more rewarding. *//*

BABCOCK WINERY & VINEYARDS // 5175 East Highway 246, Lompoc, CA 93436

T 805.736.1455
F 805.736.3886
E info@babcockwinery.com

www.babcockwinery.com

ACCESS
From Highway 101, take Highway 246 exit. Head west for about 9 miles. Winery is on right.

Hours for visits and tastings:
10:30AM–4PM, Friday–Sunday.
12–4PM, Monday.
By appointment midweek.
Closed on major holidays.

Wheelchair access.

TASTINGS & TOURS
Charge for tasting: $5 for six to eight wines. Groups of ten or more must make reservations.

No tours.

Typical wines offered: Chardonnay, Pinot Grigio, Sauvignon Blanc, Pinot Noir, Cabernet Sauvignon, and Syrah.

Wine-related items for sale.

PICNICS & PROGRAMS
No picnic area open to public.

Special events: Open house during the Vintners Festival in April and Harvest in October. Terroir Exclusives BBQ in July. Check website for dates.

Wine club.

Beckmen Vineyards

OWNER: THOMAS BECKMEN // WINEMAKER: STEVE BECKMEN

Founded in 1994, Beckmen Vineyards is a family-run winery located in the hills above Los Olivos. If you're looking for quality wines made with biodynamic farming practices, served in an idyllic setting, you've come to the right place.

Tom Beckmen, a Los Angeles businessman, so enjoyed visiting Santa Ynez Valley with his family that he decided to trade his urban life for a country one. His son Steve, a self-taught winemaker who honed his craft working with noted viticulturist Jeff Newton, was drawn to the valley's experimental spirit. The Beckmens purchased a rundown property and lovingly restored it. The ranch included an existing winery and sixteen acres of vineyards planted to Cabernet Sauvignon, Chardonnay, and Sauvignon Blanc.

The Beckmens began with a small production of some three thousand cases annually (now sixteen thousand) of Bordeaux and Rhône varietals made from both estate and purchased fruit. They soon started looking for additional land so that they could farm more of their own grapes and purchase fewer from other sources. In 1996, they acquired an unplanted hillside property in nearby Ballard Canyon, naming it Purisima Mountain Vineyard. Overlooking the Santa Ynez Valley, the sprawling 375-acre ranch is ideal for Rhône varietals, due to the limestone subsoil and microclimate. Limestone soil – a rarity in California, but commonly found in France's Rhône region – is not easily penetrated by plant roots. As a result, the plants are less vigorous and produce smaller vines, but yield intensely concentrated fruit. The property's elevation of 1,250 feet, combined with marine air from the Pacific Ocean, proved beneficial as well. Of the entire property, 125 acres are planted to Rhône varietals along with some Cabernet Sauvignon and Sauvignon Blanc. Conceived by Steve as a "palette of small vineyards," the plantings follow the sensual contours of the hillsides in a mosaic-like pattern.

In 2003, the Beckmens began farming biodynamically in the Purisima Mountain Vineyard. The biodynamic agricultural movement, started in 1924 by German philosopher and educator Rudolf Steiner, recognizes the essential qualities and rhythms of nature, in particular the movement and alignment of the planets and stars. In practice, biodynamic farming uses composting to ensure healthy soil, and natural, rather than chemical, methods of deterring pests. Following the annual biodynamic calendar, Steve Beckmen determines the ideal time for planting, plowing, and harvesting. Nine special preparations made from such organic materials as cow manure and weeds, like horsetail and dandelion, serve as compost or sprays for pest control and for nurturing the soil and plants. Beckmen is convinced that the results of the biodynamic method are evident in both the health of his vines and the flavor of his wines. The shoots and tips grow straight up, and the leaves curl toward the sun. Compared with other fruit, his ripens more fully, with a finer level of tannin, giving the wine an elegant character.

Arriving at the winery, along a winding driveway, you'll see three gazebos perched on the edge of a duck pond – a picture-perfect picnic spot. At the top of the driveway is a cottage housing the tasting room, surrounded by masses of lavender and rosebushes. There are olive trees on the grounds and an acre of orchard lush with apple, pomegranate, plum, and fig trees. Fuji apples can be purchased in the tasting room. From the deck outside, you'll get a view of the pond and the Syrah vineyards.

Although Beckmen produces a wide selection of Rhônes, both single varietals and blends, the winery's benchmark is its Syrah. Steve Beckmen is bullish on Syrah, a grape that can thrive in cool or warm climates, each delivering different styles of wines. The Beckmen Syrahs are bottled under six different labels and are produced from estate (Beckmen Vineyards) and Purisima Mountain Vineyard fruit. While the estate Syrah exudes lush blueberry and blackberry notes, the Purisima is earthy with wood, spice, and blackberry notes. The tasting lineup will take you through a tropical Sauvignon Blanc; an aromatic Marsanne; a Cuvée Le Bec, a silky blend of Syrah, Mourvèdre, and Counoise; a Le Bec Blanc, a clean, crisp blend of Marsanne, Roussanne, and Grenache Blanc; a deep, rich Cabernet Sauvignon from Purisima Mountain Vineyard; and a refreshingly crisp Grenache Rosé, perfect for a summer afternoon.

At the end of your visit, stop by the pond and relax in the tranquility that surrounds the Beckmen garden. Savor a glass of the Purisima Mountain Syrah and take a moment to ponder the cosmic forces that have played an integral part in the creation of this fine wine. ⌒

BECKMEN VINEYARDS // 2670 Ontiveros Road, P.O. Box 542, Los Olivos, CA 93441

T 805.688.8664
F 805.688.9983
E info@beckmenvineyards.com

www.beckmenvineyards.com

ACCESS
From Highway 101, take Highway 154 exit east toward Santa Barbara. After 4 miles, turn right on Roblar Avenue. Take second left, onto Ontiveros Road, and follow sign to winery.

Hours for visits and tastings:
11AM – 5PM daily.
Closed on major holidays.

Wheelchair access.

TASTINGS & TOURS
Charge for tasting: $5 for five to seven wines.

Tours by appointment only.

Typical wines offered: Syrah, Grenache, red Rhône blend, white Rhône blend, Marsanne, Roussanne, Sauvignon Blanc, and Cabernet Sauvignon.

Wine-related items for sale.

PICNICS & PROGRAMS
Picnic area open to visitors to Beckmen tasting room. Wine club members can reserve gazebo in advance. No picnic ingredients sold in tasting room. Pick up a picnic lunch at Panino Café in Los Olivos.

Special events: Annual wine club party in August; open house in April and October. Check website for event calendar.

Wine club.

Buttonwood Farm Winery & Vineyard

OWNERS: BRET DAVENPORT, SEYBURN ZORTHIAN & BARRY ZORTHIAN
WINEMAKER: MICHAEL BROWN

Buttonwood Farm Winery & Vineyard grew out of one woman's vision. Louisiana native Betty Williams, who had moved to Pasadena with her artist husband Jirayr Zorthian, wished to raise their three children in the safe haven of California's countryside. Following her divorce, the enterprising matriarch, who had a love for horses and a desire to work with the land, purchased the Buttonwood horse ranch in 1968. She renamed it Buttonwood Farm and embarked on breeding thoroughbred horses. A consummate activist (her younger days were flavored with Southern politics dominated by the likes of the legendary populist Huey Long), Williams helped shape Santa Ynez development and co-founded The Land Trust for Santa Barbara County. By the early 1980s, Williams sensed the winegrowing opportunity in the area. At the suggestion of Michael Benedict (co-partner in the famed Sanford & Benedict Vineyards), who saw potential in the farm's rolling hillsides with its exposure to the sun and rocky loam soil, Williams made the switch from horses to vineyards. In 1983, with the help of son-in-law Bret Davenport, she planted thirteen acres (later expanded to thirty-nine acres) of Bordeaux varietals up on a mesa of the 106-acre property. The lower fourteen acres that had been used for horse operations were converted to an organic fruit and vegetable farm.

Basking in her eighty-something years, Williams has retired from the business, now owned by her daughters Seyburn and Barry Zorthian and her son-in-law Davenport. A professional artist, Seyburn, who studied in Japan, is the creative mind behind Buttonwood's Asian-inspired labels. The brush stroke images done in Sumi ink are an abstract representation of the grapevines. A hayloft in the adjacent barn serves as Seyburn's studio, where she also conducts art classes.

The Buttonwood Farm property is divided between the lower part, where the tasting room is located, and the higher mesa, home to the winery and the Williams residence. Built in 1989, the twelve-hundred-square-foot winery (it was the 19th bonded winery in Santa Barbara County) initially produced five hundred cases annually. It has now expanded to 7,400 square feet with an annual production of eighty-five hundred cases. Initially the wine was sold through distributors and mail order until the family recognized the potential of the Alamo Pintado corridor. In 1992, a farm stand–cum–tasting room structure was built, with produce sold on one side of the room and wines on the other. After three years, the produce stand was discontinued and the farmhouse building officially converted to a tasting room. Williams turned over the management of the two-hundred-tree peach orchard and the two-acre vegetable lot to others who share their proceeds with Buttonwood Farm. The peaches are sold from one of the barns adjacent to the tasting room, and the vegetables go to local restaurants. The garden holds other fruit trees, such as persimmons, pears, and pomegranates, which are consumed by the Williams family.

Although Buttonwood Farm produces more red wine than white, it's best known for its Sauvignon Blanc. "We are a Santa Barbara anomaly, in that we don't have Pinot Noir or Chardonnay," asserts Davenport. And there are no plans to produce these varietals. However, Syrah and Marsanne have been added to a vineyard planted primarily to Bordeaux varietals such as Cabernet Sauvignon, Cabernet Franc, Merlot, Sauvignon Blanc, and Semillon. Although located on the eastern part of Santa Ynez Valley known for its warm temperature, the vineyards experience a milder climate. "We are in the cooler hot area," muses Davenport. Because of its elevation and exposure to the sun, the region heats up slowly in the morning and cools down faster in the afternoon, as opposed to neighboring vineyards that seem to retain more heat in the late afternoon.

"We are the last ones to pick our fruit in this region," notes Davenport. The long hang time on the vine helps balance the acidity and develop the fruit's ripe flavors. Hence, Buttonwood Farm delivers a wine that is austere but shows elegant fruit and is considerably low in alcohol. "Our wines are generally well balanced with distinct tannins," comments Davenport. "They are not fruit bombs driven by high alcohol."

A keen surfer, Michael Brown, Buttonwood Farm's winemaker, started in the wine industry by removing shoots from the vines in his native Australia. He moved to California, earned a master's degree at UC Davis in 1981, and honed his winemaking skills at such wineries as Mosby, Zaca Mesa, and the Santa Ynez Valley Winery. Brown, who wears two hats as owner/winemaker of the Kalyra label, began consulting with Buttonwood Farm in 1989 and came on board full-time in 1991. Brown started the Kalyra label early on while working at other wineries and using their facilities. In 2002, he took over the former Santa Ynez Valley Winery and turned it into a Kalyra tasting room. Brown produced his Kalyra wines at Buttonwood Farm facility until 2004.

Commenting on Buttonwood Farm's Bordeaux blends, Brown places them more in the style of fine Bordeaux wine than Napa Valley wines, which he finds to be too tannic and high in alcohol. "Our wines have softer tannins, nice aromatics, and a richer mouthfeel," says the winemaker, who shuns heavily oaked

---

BUTTONWOOD FARM WINERY & VINEYARD // 1500 Alamo Pintado Road, Solvang, CA 93463

T 805.688.3032
F 805.688.6168
E info@buttonwoodwinery.com

www.buttonwoodwinery.com

ACCESS
From Highway 101, take Highway 246 exit and turn right, go through Solvang to Alamo Pintado Road. Turn left, go approximately 1 mile. Winery is on right.

Hours open for visits and tastings:
11AM–5PM daily.
Closed on major holidays.

Wheelchair access.

TASTINGS & TOURS
Charge for tasting: $7.50 for seven to ten wines. Includes logo glass.

No tours.

Typical wines offered: Sauvignon Blanc, Merlot, Cabernet Sauvignon, Cabernet Franc, Syrah, Marsanne, and blends.

Wine-related items for sale.

PICNICS & PROGRAMS
Picnic area open to public. No picnic ingredients sold in tasting room. Pick up lunch at one of the cafes in Los Olivos.

Special events: Louisiana-style crawfish boil in May, Red White & Blues concert in June; peach harvest celebration in July; open house in April and October; and winemaker dinners. Check website for dates.

Wine club.

---

wines. Brown uses less new oak and more of neutral barrels that are three to four years old. He is not keen on the strong barrel aromas overpowering the grape's flavor. "I'd much rather concentrate on what comes from the vineyard," says the purist winemaker.

Brown's streamlined style is reflected in the velvety Syrah, redolent with aromas of black berries. His Australian touch extends to the Syrah–Cabernet Sauvignon blend, a wine that marries the spicy notes of Syrah to the rich plum flavors of Cabernet. The single varietal Cabernet Sauvignon is aged in oak barrels for two years and echoes with chocolate aromas and soft tannins. Trevin, the Bordeaux style blend, combines Cabernet Sauvignon with Merlot and Cabernet Franc so that it exudes a warm earthy richness with firm tannins. Although single varietal Cabernet Franc is not commonly seen in most tasting rooms, at Buttonwood Farm this medium body wine is bottled as Infant and delivers raspberry flavors laced with dark chocolate. Red Hawk, a blend of Cabernet Sauvignon and Cabernet Franc, is named after the winged partners that circle the vineyard at harvest time, discouraging grape-eating starlings from ravaging the vines. As an alternative to Chardonnay, Buttonwood's white lineup includes the flagship Sauvignon Blanc that rings with pear and citrus notes. A variation on the Sauvignon Blanc theme, Devin is blended with Semillon. A year of barrel aging gives the wine a creamy mouth-feel while maintaining the refreshing tropical notes. A new addition to the white family, though produced in small quantities, is Marsanne, a wine lush with figs and pear notes that makes for a perfect summer wine.

Named after the tree that anchors the tasting room, Buttonwood Farm is the first winery on Alamo Pintado Road as you turn off Highway 246. A lush fruit orchard encircles the tasting room, and the Williams-designed garden is accented by sculptor Warren Wellman's Agrisculptures—whimsical pieces crafted from rusty old farm implements. These sculptures continue inside the intimate tasting room, in the form of lamps and a wagon wheel hanging from the ceiling. An additional tasting counter on the patio accommodates imbibers on weekends. Benches are scattered around the garden, where you can relax and take in the fragrance wafting from matriarch Williams' wildflower meadow.

Honoring their Welsh heritage, Barbara Banke and her husband Jess Jackson named their winery Cambria, the Roman name for Wales, when they acquired the original Tepusquet Vineyard. The property, planted in the early 1970s, was purchased by Banke and Jackson in 1986. A year later they established Cambria, and in 1988 harvested the first vintage.

The approach to Cambria takes you through the backroads of Foxen Canyon Trail, into the heart of vineyard country and the historic Santa Maria Bench. Turning on Santa Maria Mesa Road, you will come across a sign on your left for Tepusquet Road and, in the distance, the famed Bien Nacido Vineyards. The three-mile drive to Cambria Estates is flanked by Bien Nacido Vineyards and Cambria's renowned Julia's Vineyards, named after Jackson and Banke's youngest daughter. Driving uphill on Chardonnay Lane, aptly named for acres of this varietal, you'll see Katherine's Vineyards, honoring their eldest daughter. Cambria's third noted vineyard, Tepusquet, lies on the easternmost part of the estate on a downward slope that protects the vines from Santa Maria's notoriously fierce winds.

The name Tepusquet reflects the area's history. The six-mile-long Santa Maria benchland (an intermediary between the Sierra Madre Mountains and the Sisquoc River), where the winery is located, was originally known as Tepuzli, a native Chumash Indian word meaning "copper coin." It was later renamed Tepusquet by the Spanish settlers. What is now known as Rancho Tepusquet was part of an 1838 Mexican land grant. Raising cattle and growing row crops were the ranch's main activities, but the Olivera family, the area's original settlers and owners of the rancho, planted some mission grapes.

Cambria produces three signature wines: the lush, tropical Katherine's Chardonnay; the rich and velvety Tepusquet Syrah; and the flagship, Julia's Pinot Noir, which delivers ripe cherry and strawberry flavors with undertones of cinnamon and spice. Of the 1,400 acres planted in the Santa Maria appellation, these three vineyards yield 90 percent of the winery's production. Another 6 percent is produced from the newer vineyards: Bench Break Vineyard and Rae's. The remaining 4 percent is set aside for experimental vineyards.

Of the five vineyards at Cambria Estate, Julia's Vineyard enjoys such a stellar reputation that a number of wineries source their Pinot Noir fruit from Julia's. Fondly dubbed Julia's Gang, these winemakers include Lane Tanner (Lane Tanner Wines), Dick Doré and Bill Wathen (Foxen), Frank Ostini and Gray Hartley (Hartley-Ostini Hitching Post), and Benjamin Silver (Benjamin Silver Wines). They are so passionate about Julia's fruit that they personally tend their own designated lots throughout the season.

Cambria's vineyards enjoy a mild temperature as a result of coastal influences from the Pacific Ocean, fifteen miles to the west. This moderate climate helps extend the growing season, allowing for extra hang time on the vine, which in turn helps balance the acidity and develop the fruit's ripe flavors. Perched at an elevation of 400 to 800 feet, the vineyards on the Santa Maria Bench are planted in sandy porous soil that was once a riverbed composed of ancient alluvial soil deposits, remnants of the nearby Sisquoc River. The shallow and porous soil allows for good drainage, which restricts vine vigor and thus forces the vine to concentrate on fruit development. Winemaker Denise Shurtleff's philosophy is all about preserving the aromas and characteristics of the grapes. "Wine is made in the vineyards," she says, and she directs the vineyard's efforts to get the best-quality grapes exhibiting the characteristics of this region. Leaf thinning is done to allow more sunlight on the grapes, which encourages full ripening; underdeveloped fruit is plucked off the vine at the verasion phase (when grapes soften and accumulate sugar) to promote the growth of densely flavored clusters. "This way, when the grapes come into the winery, we don't overprocess the juice," says Shurtleff.

The tasting room and the winery building appear to be dwarfed by the large stainless-steel tanks standing guard at the entrance. The inviting patio with a panoramic view leads to the expansive tasting room. Inside, the entryway is graced with a display of photographs depicting the barrel-making process. Also on display are a couple of barrels in different stages of construction, along with a wood sample from France's Allier forest. The concrete-topped bar sits in front of a large window overlooking Katherine's Vineyard; two more windows offer a view of the barrel room. A cozy lounge area anchored by a fireplace and furnished with leather sofas makes a comfortable spot to relax and savor Cambria's wines.

Before you say "*da boch*" (Welsh for "goodbye") to Cambria, take in the panorama from the hilltop: Foxen Canyon lies to the east, Santa Maria to the west, and, on a clear day, the Pacific Ocean comes into view. In springtime, the hillsides are awash with bursts of wildflowers, and in the fall, as the vine leaves turn color, the vineyards glisten with shades of gold, yellow, and vibrant oranges. //

52

CAMBRIA ESTATE VINEYARD & WINERY // 5475 Chardonnay Lane, Santa Maria, CA 93454

T 805.937.8091
F 805.934.3589
E info@cambriawines.com

www.cambriawines.com

ACCESS
From Highway 101, take Betteravia exit. Go east 7.4 miles to fork in road. Turn left on Santa Maria Mesa Road, continue 3.6 miles, and turn left on Chardonnay Lane.

Hours for visits and tastings:
10AM – 5PM daily.
Closed on major holidays.

Wheelchair access.

TASTINGS & TOURS
Charge for tasting: $5.

Tours by appointment only.

Typical wines offered: Chardonnay, Viognier, Pinot Noir, and Syrah.

Wine-related items for sale.

PICNICS & PROGRAMS
Picnic area open to public.
Picnic ingredients sold in tasting room.

Special events: Open house during Vintners' Festival in April and Harvest Festival in October. Check website for dates.

Wine club.

Fess Parker Winery & Vineyard

OWNERS: ELI PARKER & ASHLEY PARKER SNIDER // WINEMAKER: BLAIR FOX
DIRECTOR OF WINEMAKING: ELI PARKER

The tasting room of the Fess Parker Winery & Vineyard may be the only place in the region where you can find coonskin caps alongside wine paraphernalia. That's because actor-turned-vintner Fess Parker is best known for his portrayal of frontiersmen in two television series, *Davy Crockett* and *Daniel Boone*, in which he sported raccoon pelts. The theme is continued in the various items displayed throughout the tasting room, though you won't find Parker wearing such a hat if you see him on the winery grounds.

How did this veteran actor of stage, television, and film get into the wine business? The short answer: his house fell off a cliff. In the mid-1980s, once their children were grown, Fess and his wife, Marcy, decided to downsize. The Parkers sold their family home and at Fess's prompting purchased a Santa Barbara beach house on a bluff. Marcy, who preferred to move to the desert, was displeased with the property and announced that she would help renovate it, but refused to spend a single night there. Something didn't sit well with her, though she couldn't say what it was. This was 1986, one of the years El Niño drenched California. The remodeling was completed, but before the house was inhabited, flooding caused it to slip off the cliff. Fess often jokes that he was both homeless and without a job.

The next year, Fess purchased the 714-acre ranch on Foxen Canyon Road. "Fess is from Texas, so he can't do anything small," explains his daughter, Ashley, the winery's vice-president. A year later, vineyards were planted with the intention of selling grapes to other producers. "But things have a way of taking on a life of their own," Ashley notes, and in 1989 the winery's first release was produced. Today, the winery produces more than 100,000 cases annually: 65,000 under the Fess Parker label, 25,000 under Parker Station, and 8,000 with a label called Frontier Red, an affordable screw-top Rhône blend for the beach crowd.

The Parkers' son, Eli, was originally in charge of supervising the planting and construction of the winery, but his desire to try his hand at winemaking led him to viticulture classes at the University of California at Davis. He also gained hands-on experience apprenticing with noted winemaker Jed Steele. He made his debut as a winemaker at Fess Parker Winery with the 1995 vintage. Eli now serves as the winery's president and director of winemaking,

working closely with winemakers Blair Fox and Brett Escalera.

Fess Parker farms some seven hundred acres of vineyards spread over four different sites: Rodney's, Marcella's, Ashley's, and Camp 4. Rodney's Vineyard, the first developed by the Parker family, is named after the Parkers' late son-in-law and is planted primarily to Rhône varietals. Then in 1995, Parker bought a portion of the famed Sierra Madre Vineyard and renamed it after his wife. The Santa Maria Valley vineyard, in proximity to cool Pacific breezes, produces Chardonnay and Pinot Noir. Although Ashley's Vineyard in Santa Rita Hills has been sold, the Parkers have a long-term contract to purchase fruit through 2011. The newest addition, Camp 4 Vineyard, is closer to the winery in the Santa Ynez Valley.

An acre of lushly landscaped gardens surrounds the winery, framed by a dramatic backdrop of oak-studded rolling hills. The spacious grounds serve as an ideal venue for various year-round activities, ranging from harvest and vintners' weekend soirees to wine club dinners and the New Release BBQ, a two-day event held in May and always attended by Fess. Come Get Your Hands Dirty allows forty wine-club members to experience the winemaking process, from grape picking to pressing and punchdown. The weekend package includes hospitality at the Fess Parker Country Inn & Spa in Los Olivos, meals, and a closing-night barbecue dinner.

The tasting room, with high ceilings and flagstone floors, is well appointed with comfortable sofas grouped around a blazing fireplace. On occasion, this room serves as a venue for intimate dinners. The shop carries plenty of Parker memorabilia, and the wine tasting is conducted by friendly staff members who often make food-pairing suggestions with the wines they pour. The white wines range from Ashley's Vineyard Sauvignon Blanc, with flavors of peach and grapefruit, to Chardonnay from Marcella's Vineyard, a wine that exudes hints of butterscotch and ripe apple. The Santa Barbara County Viognier shows hints of citrus and honeysuckle, and the jammy American Tradition Reserve Syrah from Rodney's Vineyard bursts with the flavor of ripe blackberries and a touch of spice. The newest addition to the Syrah portfolio is Mackie's. Named after Fess's mother, this approachable and uncomplicated wine is blended with small amounts of Mourvèdre, Grenache, and Carignane.

Winery tours are by appointment and scheduled every two hours, starting at 11AM. The thirty-minute tour – which might last longer if Fess is conducting it – will take you through the barrel room, production facility, and vineyards. As you take in the panoramic vineyard scene from the stone-draped veranda, you might ask yourself, where else could you come across videotapes of *Old Yeller* and *Davy Crockett* at a winery? Or better yet, a raccoon-topped bottle stopper? //

FESS PARKER WINERY & VINEYARD // 6200 Foxen Canyon Road, Los Olivos, CA 93441

T 805.688.1545
F 805.686.1130
E sharilyn@fessparker.com

www.fessparker.com

ACCESS
From Highway 101, exit 154/Zaca Station Road. Head east and turn left on Zaca Station Road. Go 4.5 miles. Winery is on right.

Hours for visits and tastings:
11AM–5PM Monday–Friday,
10AM–5PM Saturday–Sunday.
Closed on major holidays.

Wheelchair access.

TASTINGS & TOURS
Charge for tasting: $7.

Tours by appointment only.

Typical wines offered: Chardonnay, Pinot Noir, Viognier, Syrah, and White Riesling.

Wine-related items for sale.

PICNICS & PROGRAMS
Picnic area open to public.
Picnic ingredients sold in tasting room.

Special events: Check website for event calendar.

Wine club.

Foxen Vineyard

OWNERS: DICK DORÉ & BILL WATHEN // WINEMAKER: BILL WATHEN

Driving down the scenic Foxen Canyon Road, you could easily miss Foxen Vineyard's shack. It's hard to imagine a more humble home for such rich, flavorful wines. Look for a large white early American clapboard house a few feet to the north and across from the winery. Then you will notice flower-filled barrels and Foxen's sign handwritten on a rough-hewn board. Trees surround the Foxen shack: deciduous oaks, locusts lush with white blooms in spring, a willow draping a nearby creek, and eucalyptuses planted in the 1800s as a wind break.

Foxen's rustic, romantic past is reflected in the ramshackle feel of the tasting room, once a blacksmith shop. The property has been in co-owner Dick Doré's family since the early 1800s. His great-great-grandfather, William Benjamin Foxen, was an English sea captain who sailed to Santa Barbara and fell in love with Eduarda Osune, the youngest daughter of regional governor Signor Osune. The captain was so smitten by Eduarda that he sold his ship, married her, and converted to Catholicism. As a result of this marriage, Foxen was allowed to purchase land. He acquired Rancho Tinaquaic in 1837 and became the first non-Spaniard to own a Mexican land grant. Captain Foxen kept his seafaring memories alive by using an anchor as the brand for the ranch's cattle and sheep. It is now the winery logo.

Foxen Winery is just one part of the two-thousand-acre Rancho Tinaquaic. In its early days, the ranch spanned the only north-south stagecoach route in the region. The white house, where both Doré and his mother Ramona were born, was a stagecoach stop and country store. It is currently used for family gatherings.

A sixth-generation Santa Barbara resident, Dick Doré worked as a banker in the late 1960s and the 1970s. When his ancestral wanderlust kicked in, he gave up his nine-to-five job, moved his family to Europe, and traveled through France, Spain, and Italy, where he developed a love for wine. His life came full circle when he decided to return to his roots and to historic Foxen Canyon. Exploring the possibilities in the wine industry, Doré worked at Rancho Tepusquet Mesa Vineyards, where he met Bill Wathen, a Central Coast native. A graduate of California Polytechnic State University, San Luis Obispo, with a degree in fruit science, Wathen had specialized in vineyard management and worked with such California pioneers as Dick Graff, founder of Chalone Vineyards, from whom he learned traditional French techniques and a minimalist approach to winemaking.

Doré and Wathen, fondly known as the Foxen Boys, formed their alliance and set up a winery in a small house adjacent to where Doré was born. They produced their first vintage in 1985 with a couple of barrels of Cabernet Sauvignon. The winery and tasting room were later moved to the current location, and the barrel room was set up in the barn, which dates to 1885. The barrel room is tiny. Jenny Williamson Doré, Dick's wife, wonders if someday they might build a better facility but admits people like to come to the shack, play with the dogs, and enjoy the rustic Foxen experience.

The tasting shack is nothing more than a small bar counter and a funky shrine loaded with odds and ends, such as photographs, memorabilia, and cartoon strips collected over the years. A small winery with an annual production of ten thousand cases, Foxen concentrates on vineyard-designated wines – those made with grapes from a single vineyard, as opposed to those from a combination of vineyards. You'll taste some very good Cabernet Sauvignon from the Tinaquaic Vineyard, or Vogelzang Vineyard in Happy Canyon in the eastern Santa Ynez Valley. Located in the foothills adjacent to Los Padres National Forest, Happy Canyon experiences the warmest temperatures in the valley and is fast gaining a reputation for its Bordeaux varietals. But it's the signature Pinot Noirs that draw regulars to Foxen. Three of the Pinot Noirs come from Julia's Vineyard, Santa Maria Valley, and the prestigious Bien Nacido Vineyard's Block 8, planted especially for Foxen. A small two-hundred-case production of Pinot Noir is from the prized Seasmoke Vineyard in Santa Rita Hills. The Dorés intend to increase the winery's Rhône program, and their newest vineyard, the Williamson Doré Vineyard, is planted to Syrah, Mourvèdre, and Grenache. Foxen also produces a small production of Sangiovese Volpino (meaning "little fox") blended with Merlot, an ideal accompaniment to pasta dishes.

Your tasting experience will take you through Foxen's signature Chenin Blanc, fragrant with honeysuckle and pear flavors; the Tinaquaic Vineyard Chardonnay, aromatic with pineapple and grapefruit; and the silky smooth vineyard-designated Pinot Noir. While savoring these wines, you might see Doré or Wathen tinkering with equipment behind the shack. They are the ones wearing the wine-stained T-shirts. In between tastings, you can relax on the inviting deck, a popular spot for the Foxen team's special Santa Maria–style barbecues, hosted during harvest and vintners' festivals, or whenever the winemakers feel up to it.

FOXEN VINEYARD // 7200 Foxen Canyon Road, Santa Maria, CA 93454

T 805.937.4251
F 805.934.0415
E foxenwine@aol.com

www.foxenvineyard.com

ACCESS
From Highway 101, take Highway 154 exit. Follow Foxen Canyon Road for 17 miles. Winery is on right.

Hours for visits and tastings:
11AM–4PM daily.
Closed on major holidays.

Wheelchair access.

TASTINGS & TOURS
Charge for tasting: Two levels of tasting at $5 and $7; includes glass.

Tours by appointment only.

Typical wines offered: Chenin Blanc, Tinaquaic Vineyard Chardonnay, various single-vineyard Pinot Noirs and Syrahs, Foothills Reserve (Merlot/Cabernet Franc blend), and a number of limited tasting-room-exclusive wines.

Wine-related items for sale.

PICNICS & PROGRAMS
No picnic ingredients sold in tasting room.

Special events: Foxen Canyon Wine Trail events, Christmas on the Trail, and Spring Passport Weekend. Check website for event calendar.

Wine club.

Gainey Vineyard

OWNER: DANIEL GAINEY // WINEMAKER: KIRBY ANDERSON

Prepare yourself for a unique educational experience at Gainey. The winery has set aside half an acre as a Visitors' Education Vineyard, with plantings of Merlot, Chardonnay, Cabernet Sauvignon, and Riesling. Thirty-minute tours cover the various grape varietals and the trellis systems in the vineyard, as well as the winery's history. Near the vineyard, displayed along a covered walkway, you'll view an impressive gallery of photographs depicting vine development throughout the season, from budbreak, flowering, and foliage to bottling. During the harvest, you are encouraged to pick the grapes in the education vineyard, taste the fruit, and compare the flavors with those of the corresponding wines.

From the vineyard, you proceed to the crush pad, the fermentation room, and the barrel room for an opportunity to learn the intricacies of barrel making. The tour's next stop is the bottle-aging room, where some twelve hundred bottles rest for a minimum of six months. The unlabeled bottles are carefully categorized by winemaker Kirby Anderson, waiting for just the right moment to be pulled out for their release.

At the end of the tour, you arrive back at the tasting room and are ready to sip Gainey's wines. The Spanish-style room is dominated by two large elk-antler chandeliers. A counter at the entrance holds a row of recipe cards with wine-pairing suggestions. Be sure to take these recipes and winemaker notes so you can re-create the Gainey experience at home. (The wine and food program stages wine-pairing dinners every six weeks with local chef Tim Neenan of the neighboring El Rancho Market.) Gourmet foods, such as tapenades, sauces, cheeses, and smoked meats, are available if you want to enjoy a picnic in the garden. Be sure to sample Martini Madness: a mixture of green-tinted white-chocolate-covered almonds and chocolate-covered dried apricots.

Of Gainey's thirteen bottlings, the tasting lineup usually includes six to eight wines ranging from Riesling, Sauvignon Blanc, and Chardonnay to Cabernet Sauvignon, Merlot, Syrah, and Pinot Noir. Anderson's Riesling is dry, with hints of citrus and green apple, and the Sauvignon Blanc, which is blended with a little Semillon, tingles the palate with flavors of pineapple. The Chardonnay, a blend of grapes from Santa Maria Valley and Santa Rita Hills, shows tropical notes with just a touch of oak.

Historically, Gainey has been known for its barrel-fermented Sauvignon Blanc (as opposed to the popular steel-vat fermentation). When Anderson came on board in the late 1990s, he expanded the red wine program and introduced Limited Selection Merlot, a wine with smooth tannins and deep berry aromas. Anderson's wine-making philosophy is simple: "I make the wine from grapes that I'm given. I don't try to force the wine to be something it's not." He spends a lot of time in the vineyard during harvest, tasting grapes to ensure they are picked at perfect ripeness. To this end, Anderson relies as much on his taste buds as he does on the Brix level, the measure of sugar content of grapes.

The Gainey family has been farming in the Santa Ynez Valley for more than forty years, and their ranch is well known as the largest diversified operation in the valley. Dan C. Gainey and his son Dan J. purchased the 1,800-acre property in the valley's eastern end in 1962. Of this acreage, 1,000 were devoted to cattle, 600 to farmland, and 100 to Arabian horses. Only 100 acres were dedicated to vineyards, of which 50 were planted in 1983. The winery was established a year later. The Home Ranch, location of the winery and tasting room, is in the warmest part of the valley, where the family concentrates on growing Bordeaux varietals. In the 1990s, the Gaineys expanded by purchasing a 120-acre parcel known as Evan's Ranch in the cooler appellation of Santa Rita Hills on the west side of the valley, where they could plant Pinot Noir, Chardonnay, and Syrah.

In addition to estate grapes, Gainey purchases fruit from other vineyards in the Santa Ynez and Santa Maria Valleys to augment its annual production of twenty-two thousand cases. Although the winery does not make vineyard-designated wines, single varietals are often blended with grapes from different vineyards. The 2002 Limited Selection Chardonnay, for example,

GAINEY VINEYARD // 3950 East Highway 246, Santa Ynez, CA 93460

T 805.688.0558
F 805.688.5864
E info@gaineyvineyard.com

www.gaineyvineyard.com

ACCESS
Hours for visits and tastings:
10AM–5PM daily.
Closed on major holidays.

Wheelchair access.

TASTINGS & TOURS
Charge for tasting: $5 for six wines; free tour. Groups of ten or more require a reservation and will receive a private tour at $12 per person, including a tasting of six wines.

Tours 11AM, 1, 2, and 3PM. Reservations required for groups of ten or more.

Typical wines offered: Sauvignon Blanc, Chardonnay, Merlot, Pinot Noir, and Riesling.

Wine-related items for sale.

PICNICS & PROGRAMS
Picnic area open to public. Picnic ingredients sold in tasting room.

Special events: Concerts in August, September, and October; annual crush party in September; winemaker dinners. Check website for event calendar.

Wine club.

is a blend of fruit from three vineyards: Gainey's Evan's Ranch, and purchased fruit from Huber Ranch in the Santa Rita Hills and Bien Nacido Vineyards in the Santa Maria Valley. Triada, a light-bodied Rhône-style wine, is a blend of Grenache, Syrah, Mourvèdre, and Viognier from Santa Rita Hills, Santa Maria Valley, and Happy Canyon. The signature Merlot and Sauvignon Blanc (blended in a typical Bordeaux style with a little Semillon) are both from Gainey's Home Ranch.

In addition to its wines, Gainey is known for its popular summer concerts that draw such noted performers as Rita Coolidge, Joan Baez, David Sanborn, and Arturo Sandoval. Another Gainey tradition is the annual Crush Party. This all-day event takes visitors through every aspect of harvest, including barrel tasting, barrel building, studying wine flavors through aroma, and even picking the grapes and stomping on them. A humorous touch is the Lucille Ball look-alike contest inspired by the famous grape-stomping episode of *I Love Lucy*. The afternoon ends with a barbecue paired with Gainey wines.

Before departing Gainey, take a few minutes to walk around the vine-covered arbor with its overhanging table grapes that you can pluck and taste. Then stroll down through the garden, where you will be embraced by the heady aroma of sage, a perfect sensory finish to your Gainey experience. ⚤

Lafond Winery & Vineyards
Santa Barbara Winery

OWNER: PIERRE LAFOND // WINEMAKER & PRESIDENT: BRUCE MᶜGUIRE

A pioneer of Santa Barbara County's wine industry, Pierre Lafond founded Santa Barbara Winery in 1962, making it the county's first post-Prohibition winery. The winery sits two blocks from Santa Barbara's pristine beaches, on Anacapa Street. The tasting room is popular with the locals, and tourists are quite surprised to find a tasting room so close to the ocean.

Starting with an annual production of one thousand cases, Santa Barbara Winery produced mostly rosé and Zinfandel. At the time, no grapes were planted in Santa Barbara County, so Lafond purchased fruit from San Luis Obispo County's York Mountain area. Later, he sourced fruit from Nielsen Vineyard (now Byron Winery), Santa Barbara County's first commercial vineyard, planted in 1964.

To maintain control over the quality of fruit, Lafond planted his first vineyard in 1972 in the rugged Santa Rita Hills: a sixty-five-acre parcel with Cabernet Sauvignon, Chardonnay, Sauvignon Blanc, Chenin Blanc, White Riesling, and Zinfandel. The vineyards were later replaced by Syrah and some Riesling, but most of the acreage was devoted to Pinot Noir, well suited to the region's cool climate. Lafond recalls the uncertainty of planting in the Santa Rita Hills: "None of us knew what kind of area this was. It was a gamble that turned out to be a good one."

With prime fruit coming from his Santa Rita Hills vineyards and an eye toward creating premium wines, Pierre Lafond launched Lafond Winery & Vineyards in 1996 with its first vintage. Located in the heart of the Santa Rita Hills, the winery and tasting room building on Santa Rosa Road was completed in 2001. Of the company's total annual production of forty thousand cases, five thousand are made under the Lafond label, with the balance under the Santa Barbara Winery label.

Lafond has ninety-five acres of vineyards in the Santa Rita Hills appellation—pure Pinot country—and has planted other varietals as well. Producing wines for both Lafond and Santa Barbara wineries, these vineyards are spread on two separate parcels on opposite sides of the Santa Ynez River, which runs north of the Lafond winery and tasting room. The thirty-acre parcel on the southern side, visible from the tasting room, is planted exclusively to Pinot Noir. The sixty-five-acre northern parcel—whose fruit is bottled under the Santa Barbara Winery label—is planted to Chardonnay, Cabernet Sauvignon, Cabernet Franc, Zinfandel, Sauvignon Blanc, and White Riesling.

Lafond Winery focuses on three varietals: Pinot Noir, Chardonnay, and Syrah. The vineyard-designated labels are produced from specific estate vineyards under the Lafond label. The Lafond Syrah expresses floral notes reminiscent of lavender and white pepper, and the silky Pinot Noir is lush with cherries. The blend of fruit from estate and other neighboring vineyards in the Santa Rita Hills is bottled under the SRH label.

A French Canadian, Lafond moved to Santa Barbara for the weather in the late 1950s. Trained as an architect, he continued this profession until 1962, when he switched to the wine business. Two years later, Lafond and his wife, Wendy Foster, opened their first retail store in Montecito, expanding to additional stores and a restaurant in Santa Barbara. Lafond's architecture background came in handy in designing the stores and Lafond Winery. You can shop for fine foods at one of the three Pierre Lafond & Company gourmet stores or dine at Pierre Lafond Bistro; purchase clothing at one of the three Wendy Foster and Angel boutiques; or pick up gifts at a home accessories and gift store. While Lafond oversees all his enterprises including the wine business, his son, David, handles vineyard management.

Lafond brought winemaker Bruce McGuire on board in 1981. McGuire's passion for winemaking was sparked in high school when a relative presented him with a home winemaking kit. Well respected in the region, McGuire is much more than a winemaker. He knows every aspect of the business, from forklift mechanics and cooperage to viticulture and running a bottling line. McGuire believes that each wine should highlight the essence and expression of the fruit unique to its vineyard. This is evident in the vineyard-designated Pinot Noir, Chardonnay, and Syrah from Lafond Vineyards.

LAFOND WINERY & VINEYARDS // 6855 Santa Rosa Road, Buellton, CA 93427

T 805.688.7921
F 805.962.4981
E lwv@lafondwinery.com

www.lafondwinery.com

ACCESS
From Highway 101, take Santa Rosa Road exit in Buellton. Go west for about 5.5 miles. Winery is on right.

Hours for visits and tastings:
10AM–5PM daily.
Closed on major holidays.

Wheelchair access.

TASTINGS & TOURS
Charge for tasting: $5 for six wines.

No tours.

Typical wines offered: Syrah, Pinot Noir, and Chardonnay.

Wine-related items for sale.

PICNICS & PROGRAMS
Picnic area open to public. No picnic ingredients sold in the tasting room. Pick up a picnic lunch from Chef's Touch in Solvang.

Special events: Winemaker dinners. Check website for event calendar.

Wine club.

In 2003, Lafond purchased Pinot Noir fruit from the neighboring Arita Hills Vineyard. A small production of this vineyard-designated wine was released in 2005.

A modern sign on a sleek wall graced with masses of lavender announces the entrance to the winery. As you pull into the parking lot, you see the Lafond Vineyards ahead. To the left, in the distance, the Santa Rita Hills come into view. The tasting room, which overlooks the barrel room, is stocked with beautifully designed gift items, such as Italian urns and fine bone and olive-wood bowls from Kenya.

To get a grand sense of the region, drive three miles west of the winery to an unmarked vista point. From here, you will have a panorama of the famed Santa Rita Hills with plantings of various noted vineyards, such as Fiddlehead, Mt. Carmel, Blind Faith, and Cargasacchi. This is pure Pinot country. ⁄⁄·

SANTA BARBARA WINERY // 202 Anacapa Street, Santa Barbara, CA 93101

T 805.963.3633
F 805.962.4981
E wine@sbwinery.com

www.sbwinery.com

ACCESS
Driving north on Highway 101, exit Garden Street. Turn right on Yanonali Street; continue a few blocks. Winery is on the right corner.

Hours for visits and tastings:
10AM – 5PM daily.
Closed on major holidays.

Wheelchair access.

TASTINGS & TOURS
Charge for tasting: $5 for six wines or more.

Tours by appointment only.

Typical wines offered: Pinot Noir, Chardonnay, Syrah, and Riesling.

Wine-related items for sale.

PICNICS & PROGRAMS
Picnic area open to public. No picnic ingredients sold in the tasting room.

Special events: Seasonal food and wine events. Check website for event calendar.

Wine club.

Melville Vineyards & Winery

OWNER: **RON MELVILLE** // WINEMAKER: **GREG BREWER**

From its first vintage in 1999, Melville's handcrafted Pinot Noirs and Chardonnays gained recognition and cult status with wine aficionados. Surprisingly, Ron Melville, a wine collector since the 1970s, had not tasted Pinot Noir till the 1990s. Melville's passion for wine, specifically Cabernet Sauvignon, began when he started collecting Napa Valley wines. Owning two seats on the Pacific Stock Exchange, he enjoyed a successful financial career until the crash of October 1987, when 40 percent of his net worth disappeared in

a matter of two hours. He made a wise decision to diversify. Since he was a wine collector, he headed to northern California and purchased a 153-acre ranch in Knight's Valley, where he grew Cabernet Sauvignon, Merlot, and Sauvignon Blanc. Knowing little about grape growing, Melville took courses at the University of California at Davis and pored over books on wine-making from different parts of the world.

For a few years, Melville sold his fruit to wineries in Napa and Sonoma. It wasn't until 1992 that he first came across a Santa Barbara wine when dining at a restaurant in Aspen, Colorado. A Cabernet Sauvignon fan, he had never tasted the Pinot Noir grape. Sipping a Pinot Noir from Au Bon Climat brought an epiphany. Melville was hooked. The grape's silky, seductive character convinced him to plant Pinot Noir vineyards. His search took him from the Russian River and Carneros in the north to Santa Ynez Valley in the south. He finally settled on the cool region of Lompoc in 1996. At that time, the neighboring Santa Rita Hills area had not been officially designated as an American Viticultural Area.

With the help of his two sons, Chad and Brent, Melville developed what is now a 139-acre parcel of Pinot Noir, Chardonnay, Syrah, and Viognier with a production of some two thousand cases per year. (A one-hundred-acre property, Verna's Vineyard in Los Alamos' Cat Canyon, has recently been added to Melville's portfolio.) Armed with his self-education

in viticulture, Ron Melville began experimenting with different clones—mutations or subdivisions of a varietal that play an important role in viticulture. Each clone of the same varietal gives the grape its individual character, which can make a noticeable difference in the wine. Pinot Noir, being a much older grape than Cabernet Sauvignon, has a greater inclination to produce mutations. After much research, Melville initially developed fourteen clones—three of Chardonnay and eleven of Pinot Noir. Now, the number of Pinot clones has expanded to fourteen and the Chardonnay to five, with an additional nine Syrah clones.

When Melville purchased the Lompoc property, his intention was to continue growing grapes for other wineries. Then he met winemaker Greg Brewer, who had heard of Melville's experiments. Brewer had left a job as French instructor at the University of California at Santa Barbara to work at Santa Barbara Winery, where he learned winemaking techniques. He started producing small amounts of Pinot Noir and Chardonnay with a partner, Steve Clifton. Brewer approached Melville and asked him to plant a section of Pinot Noir and Chardonnay especially for his Brewer-Clifton label. The two men hit it off. Melville, now motivated to build a winery, asked Brewer to come on board as winemaker while continuing to make his own wines. It was an unlikely team—a financier and a French teacher—but one that has worked extremely well from the start.

A winemaker with a cult following, the unassuming Brewer takes a minimalist approach to his work. Shunning the title "winemaker," he considers himself a steward who gently ushers the grapes on their journey from vine to bottle. He is a master of nonintervention, refraining from using what he calls "tricks of the trade." "Everything I do," he says, "is an effort not to do something." Brewer's love for Japanese cuisine and Taoism has inspired this philosophy. The true representation of the Santa Rita Hills appellation is reflected in the winery's Pinot Noirs, redolent of bright red and blue fruits; the Syrahs, bursting with dark cherry, black pepper, and cinnamon; and the clean and fresh Chardonnays, exuding flavors of orange blossom and lemon tart. The clones developed by Melville allow Brewer to arrive at these perfectly balanced flavors.

MELVILLE VINEYARDS & WINERY // 5185 East Highway 246, Lompoc, CA 93436

T 805.735.7030
F 805.735.5310
E info@melvillevineyards.com

www.melvillewinery.com

ACCESS
From Highway 101, take Highway 246 exit. Head west about 9 miles. Winery is on right.

Hours for visits and tastings:
11AM – 4PM daily.
Closed on major holidays.

Wheelchair access

TASTINGS & TOURS
Charge for tasting: $5, reimbursed with purchase.

Tours free. Groups of ten or more by appointment only.

Typical wines offered: Pinot Noir, Syrah, Chardonnay, and Viognier.

Wine-related items for sale.

PICNICS & PROGRAMS
Picnic area open to public. No picnic ingredients sold in tasting room. Pick up a picnic lunch from Chef's Touch in Solvang.

Special events: Winemaker dinner in April, Pinot Noir Symposium in May, and Harvest BBQ in November. Check website for dates.

No wine club.

Each clone has a distinctive character, and blending different clones creates levels of complexity. During a tasting here, your server will enlighten you with information about the different clones and their individual characteristics.

Melville's Mediterranean-style winery sits behind well-manicured vineyards off Highway 246. The region's cool climate, ideal for Pinot Noir and Chardonnay, prolongs the growing season. This extends the hang time for grapes on the vines, yielding fully developed grapes with an ideal balance of fruit flavor and acidity. The vineyards are planted on a north-south axis, and vine rows are tightly spaced, which stresses the vines and discourages a high yield of fruit. While most vintners traditionally speak of yields in tons of grapes per acre, the Melville mantra is pounds per acre. Only the best fruit is picked and makes its way into Melville bottles. These prized grapes are also sought out by such noted wineries as Whitcraft, Bonaccorsi, Jaffurs, and Brewer-Clifton.

The long driveway leading to the winery brings you into a parking lot surrounded by rows of Pinot Noir vines, identified by their clones. Inside the semi-circular tasting room, blue halogen lamps hang low over the tasting counter. From here, you'll get a good view of the barrel room. Your tasting experience will take you through Melville's signature Estate Pinot Noir; the Estate Clone 76 Inox (French for "stainless steel"), a flinty wine with crisp acidity; the fragrant Estate Viognier; and the velvety Estate Syrah. Melville also produces small-lot collections from specific vineyards. The High Density Pinot Noir comes from a third of an acre of vineyard that has eleven of the fourteen clones.

To fully enjoy the Melville experience, pull up a chair on the shaded terrace overlooking the vineyards and allow the Pinot Noir to linger leisurely over your palate. Now, picture the Taoist wine-steward who effortlessly ushered the temperamental Pinot Noir into a seductive wine that has rightfully gained a cult following. ☯☯

Rideau Vineyard

OWNER: IRIS DUPLANTIER-RIDEAU // WINEMAKER: ANDRÉS IBARRA

Along the scenic corridor of Alamo Pintado Road, dotted with horse ranches and apple orchards, stands the historic Alamo Pintado Adobe, home to Rideau Vineyard's winery and tasting room. Here, you'll get a good dose of Iris Duplantier-Rideau's New Orleans hospitality served against a backdrop of Santa Ynez's history.

A fringe-topped surrey sits at the entrance of the winery, which is lined with rosebushes. A porch, appointed with white wicker furniture, wraps around the adobe, which dates to 1884 and was originally part of a Spanish land grant. The property was later taken over by two English expatriates, Daniel B. W. Alexander and Fred Grundy, who turned it into a popular guest ranch and inn during the stagecoach era.

Over the years, the adobe fell into disrepair. Although the building was designated a Santa Barbara County Historical Monument in 1978, it lay in shambles – its walls riddled with woodpecker holes and its wood floors sagging – until Rideau rescued it in 1996. Rideau, a Los Angeles–based insurance and securities entrepreneur, was looking for a getaway for herself and her mother. In the 1980s, she visited the valley to attend the Vintners' Festival and fell in love with the area. Rideau found a property a short distance up the hill from the adobe, purchased it in 1989, and built two houses, for herself and her mother. When the adobe came on the market, she snatched it up. It reminded her of her grandfather's home in New Orleans.

Rideau had originally planned to turn the adobe into a bed-and-breakfast, but the property was zoned for agriculture. Her only choice was to grow grapes and use the building as a winery. She had no background in viticulture, but as luck would have it, noted winemaker Richard Longoria was looking for a place to make his wines. They teamed up, planted Rhône varietals, and got the winery up and running. At the same time, Rideau worked hard at transforming the decayed adobe into a graceful Victorian beauty. Rideau's first production in 1996 was a mere 300 cases made from purchased fruit. It wasn't until 2001 that the thirty-acre estate vineyards were planted: ten acres of Viognier, Grenache, and Mourvèdre in front of the winery, fifteen acres of Roussanne behind the winery, and five acres of Syrah up on a knoll. The winery now produces 10,000 to 12,000 cases annually, sold exclusively through the tasting room and wine club.

Visiting the Rideau tasting room is a heady experience. Every detail is beautifully executed, from the original hardwood floors to the intimate antiques-filled rooms. For the New Orleans native, owning a winery is more than making good Rhône-style wines, the winery's focus. It's also about reaching into her roots and cooking Creole specialties. For a Creole, everything revolves around food, which explains the large kitchen in the tasting room. In earlier days, when the tasting room was less busy, Rideau spent weekends turning out jambalaya, crab cakes, and gumbo, dishes that highlighted her Viogniers and Rhône blends. She now cooks for four annual events, with the help of a local chef. Held on the winery's spacious grounds, the parties also include live jazz. If you can't make one of the big events, you can experience the tasting room kitchen, which is always warm and busy. The counter is stacked with assorted mustards and delicious tapenades, which are served with baskets of fresh crusty baguettes. The kitchen walls are lined with Creole spices, bayou hot sauces, beignet mixes, and lavender products.

Rideau's multiple tasting rooms, displaying award-winning bottles, are all housed in the adobe. The main room, where you will be handed a glass and colorful strings of Mardi Gras beads, is in the tented patio. A suite of three luxuriously appointed rooms, with velvet drapes, Victorian chairs, and antique counters, is reserved for Cellar Club members. Although Rideau's wines are ready to drink, they can be cellared for a few years. Winemaker Andrés Ibarra is adept at Rhône blends as well as single varietals such as the aromatic Viognier and the award-wining Roussanne, produced in limited quantity. The tropical Fleur Blanche is a blend of Viognier and Roussanne, and the signature red Rhône blend, Château Duplantier, is loaded with caramel and blackberries. The top-of-the-line estate Syrah and Viognier bottles bear Iris's name in gold-embossed letters, designed by her artist friend Laura Schy.

As you stroll through the expansive gardens, a Vieux Carré sign points to the adobe, and jazz music pipes in through the speakers hidden inside large rocks along the walkway. The tented patio looks festive, with its inviting furniture and table-topped barrels under garden umbrellas. From the sunny porch to the jasmine-draped arbor, there are so many nooks and corners in the garden that you might spend more time than planned relishing Rideau's Southern hospitality. ⌃

RIDEAU VINEYARD // 1562 Alamo Pintado Road, Solvang, CA 93463

T 805.688.0717
F 805.688.8048
E irisrideau@verizon.com

www.rideauvineyard.com

ACCESS
From Highway 101, take Highway 246 exit and turn right. Go through Solvang to Alamo Pintado Road. Turn left and go 1 mile. Winery is on right.

Hours for visits and tastings:
11AM–5PM daily.
Closed on major holidays.

Wheelchair access.

TASTINGS & TOURS
Charge for tasting: $10 for regular tasting and $15 for reserve tasting. Both include a Riedel crystal logo glass.

No tours.

Typical wines offered: Roussanne, Viognier, Syrah, Chardonnay, Pinot Noir, Sangiovese, Riesling, and Rhône blends, both white and red.

Wine-related items for sale.

PICNICS & PROGRAMS
Picnic area open to public. Picnic ingredients sold in tasting room. For a substantial meal, pick up lunch at Panino Café in nearby Los Olivos.

Special events: Monthly Creole open house, plus Fourth of July, Iris Rideau's birthday, and Christmas parties. Check website for event calendar.

Wine club.

Rusack Vineyards

OWNERS: ALISON WRIGLEY RUSACK & GEOFFREY CLAFLIN RUSACK
WINEMAKERS: JOHN & HELEN FALCONE

Rusack Vineyards is a small jewel of a winery off the beaten path. Located a mere six-minute drive from Buellton and Solvang, it's one of the best-kept secrets of the region. The scenic drive through Ballard Canyon Road's bucolic countryside, by pristine, pricey ranches, brings you to the winery entrance, marked by bursts of poppies and wildflowers brushing against a stone wall.

A romantic ambience permeates the picture-perfect setting. A redwood deck wraps around four mature oak trees and offers a view of the vineyards and oak-studded rolling hills. You can enjoy your picnic lunch here or just savor Rusack's crisp Sauvignon Blanc on a warm summer's day. The adjoining tasting room was once a gas station; today, it is a handsomely designed space with stone floors.

Owners Geoffrey Claflin Rusack and Alison Wrigley Rusack purchased the forty-eight-acre property in 1992. The existing winery and the twenty-year-old vineyards were in shambles. The facility had been constructed without permits by the previous owners, who intended the winery and vineyards to serve as a movie set, a permissible use of the property. Films were never shot, but grapes were grown and wines were made. A lawyer by profession, Geoff Rusack worked his way through the Santa Barbara County bureaucracy to get the right permits. He also ripped out old vineyards and planted new ones. One thing he has learned is the importance of good grapes. That's why, Rusack notes, the license given to a grower is called a "wine-grower's license," not a "grape-grower's license."

Before pulling out the old vineyards, the Rusacks brought in noted Napa winemaker John Falcone. He and his wife, Helen, an enologist, moved to Ballard Canyon and set up home on a horse ranch across from the winery. The Falcones meticulously surveyed the varied soils and slopes on the property and selected the very best. By 2001, most of the estate vineyards were replanted predominantly to Syrah, a grape well suited to this region and its well-drained, sandy loam soil. Although Falcone believes that microclimate more than soil impacts the flavor of the wine, he does feel that soil affects the vine's growth. Well-drained soil that allows for less-vigorous growth gives the wine more pure fruit flavor. Certain soils, Falcone explains, are good for specific varietals, such as clay soil for Chardonnay and Pinot Noir.

The seventeen-acre vineyard also contains Grenache, Sangiovese, and Sauvignon Blanc. A minuscule section is planted to Bordeaux varietals for Rusack's limited production of Anacapa, a Bordeaux blend. The new plantings are done in a precise and scientific manner. From the deck, you can see that the vineyards are laid out so they get maximum sun exposure from east and west.

Since Ballard Canyon is wedged between the cool west side and the warmer east side of Santa Ynez Valley, it experiences a more moderate climate than other parts of the county. Although not close to the coast, the region gets some benefit of the ocean breeze, which allows for cool nights and foggy mornings, ideal for grapes to maintain healthy acid levels. Although the climate is moderate here, Falcone defines the Syrah from this region as more of a warm-climate Syrah, more fruit-forward than a true cool-climate Syrah, which exudes a spicy character with flavors of red-berry fruit. Of a total annual production of 5,000 cases, 1,200 are dedicated to estate Syrah. For its Pinot Noir production of 1,500 cases annually, Rusack purchases fruit from Garey's Vineyard and Solomon Hills in the Santa Maria Valley, and Fiddlestix and Huber in the Santa Rita Hills. For the 2,000-case annual production of Chardonnay, he sources fruit from the renowned Bien Nacido Vineyards and Foley and Rancho Santa Rosa in the Santa Rita Hills.

Changes at Rusack Vineyards have occurred beyond new vineyard plantings and the tasting room. The winery's original label–a ship at sea–was replaced by the image of a tile. The Rusacks adopted this design to honor Alison's great-grandfather William Wrigley, Jr., founder of Wrigley Chewing Gum Company, who at one time owned Santa Catalina Island. Wrigley established a building-materials company and a decorative tile and ceramics factory on the island seventy-five years ago. The ceramics business lasted only seven years, but the Catalina tile became a revered collectible.

Since Ballard Canyon is horse country, you might see local equestrians on nearby trails. Occasionally, riders take a break, tie their horses to a hitching post by the deck, and step inside for a tasting. The winery's grounds are home to many birds, including a covey of California quail, Western bluebirds, woodpeckers, and magpies. Raptors such as red-shoulder and red-tailed hawks abound, keeping vineyards free of rodents. You might even catch sight of a flock of wild turkeys roaming along Ballard Canyon. One or two occasionally wander onto the winery's grounds, surprising visitors. *//*

RUSACK VINEYARDS // 1819 Ballard Canyon Road, Solvang, CA 93463

T 805.688.1278
F 805.686.1508
E info@rusackvineyards.com

www.rusackvineyards.com

ACCESS
From Highway 101, take Highway 246 exit. Turn right and go .75 mile through Buellton. Turn left on Ballard Canyon Road and continue to T intersection, then turn left. Winery is 2 miles on left.

Hours for visits and tastings:
11AM–5PM daily.
Closed on major holidays.

Wheelchair access.

TASTINGS & TOURS
Charge for tasting: $6; includes logo glass.

Free tours. Groups of ten or more by appointment only.

Typical wines offered: Sauvignon Blanc, Chardonnay, Pinot Noir, Syrah, Cabernet Franc, Sangiovese, and Anacapa, a Bordeaux blend.

Wine-related items for sale.

PICNICS & PROGRAMS
Picnic area open to public. Picnic ingredients sold in tasting room. For a substantial meal, pick up a picnic lunch in Solvang or Buellton.

Special events: Check website for event calendar.

Wine club.

A touch of Provence awaits you at Sunstone Vineyards & Winery, as you drive up the dirt road straddled by rows of Merlot vineyards. Inspired by her trips to southern France, Linda Rice has captured that timeless country ambience: the scents of lavender and rosemary perfume the air, and vine-draped arbors abound in the courtyard that hugs the winery, which is awash in the sun-drenched colors of Provence. Linda and Fred Rice moved to Santa Ynez in 1989 with their children to grow grapes and enjoy the country life. Four years later,

they established the winery, giving it a name that refers to the region's bountiful sunshine and the faux stone specially crafted for the winery. The winery and tasting room were originally housed in the former horse barn. After an oak tree fell on the building during a rainstorm, the Rices created the Provençal-style winery and tasting room.

The Rice family is committed to organic farming on its 103-acre estate. Their vineyard is currently the only state-certified organic one in the region. The terraced site of Sunstone estate provides habitat for owls, bats, hawks, and gopher snakes, which control the population of gophers, ground squirrels, and rodents. Clover and other cover crops, planted intermittently among the rows of vines, compete with the vines, causing maximum flavor concentration in the grapes. The crops are also vital for supporting beneficial insects such as ladybugs (they catch aphids) and spiders (they go for leafhoppers). Daniel Gehrs, veteran winemaker and Sunstone consultant, believes that the toxin-free soil (a combination of sand, gravel, and loam on the surface and deeply rooted Monterey shale) captures the essence of *terroir*: the specific site whose soil, slope, and climatic conditions give a grape its individual character and produce strong vines with healthy immune systems. Sunstone is known for its Rhône varietals and a few Bordeaux blends. The deep crimson Rapsodie du Soleil is a Cote-du-Rhône-style blend of Syrah and Mourvèdre with a touch of Viognier.

Sunterra and Eros are blends of Cabernet Sauvignon, Merlot, and Cabernet Franc. Single-varietal wines include Syrah, Chardonnay, Sauvignon Blanc, and an aromatic Viognier.

On entering Sunstone, you will hear the soothing sound of water trickling from a Romanesque fountain. Visitors can gather under patio umbrellas to enjoy their picnic lunches in this glorious farmhouse setting. Once inside the tasting room, they gravitate toward the country-style kitchen, where appetizers are served on weekends and paired with Sunstone wines.

The five-thousand-square-foot stone winery's special feature is the 280-foot-deep cave with three chambers dug into the hillsides. Two caves hold library wines and old vintages, and the middle Cuvée cave is used for special events and production and on weekends and holidays serves as a tasting room. The caves form an ideal backdrop for Sunstone's year-round entertaining. There's the holiday open house, Valentine's Day and harvest celebration dinners, the Wild West BBQ, and the Club Sunstone harvest stomp party. For certain events, wrought-iron chandeliers illuminated with candles are installed.

Sunstone is popular on weekends. A tasting counter is set up in the courtyard to accommodate the crowd. You might see jays, sparrows, and woodpeckers amid the bursts of lavender. The demonstration kitchen is busy with people nibbling on mini pizzas and freshly baked breads. The cooking is usually done by local chefs, although at times one of the Rices' two daughters, Brittney, a Cordon Bleu–trained chef and a budding winemaker, comes from San Francisco to take over the kitchen.

On weekdays, the kitchen counter is transformed into the Essence Table, where a sip-and-smell exercise takes you through the various characteristics of wine. On one day, the featured wine was Sunstone's Eros, a blend of Cabernet Sauvignon, Cabernet Franc, and Merlot. Displayed with the wine was an assortment of ingredients – vanilla, chocolate, blueberries, cherries, plums, currants, and tobacco – the key flavors and aromas associated with that wine. Visitors were encouraged to smell each ingredient and identify its presence in the wine.

A few miles away, the Rices' son, Bion, has set up his own boutique label, Artiste, which can be sampled

SUNSTONE VINEYARDS & WINERY // 125 Refugio Road, Santa Ynez, CA 93460

T 805.688.9463
F 805.688.1881
E club@sunstonewinery.com

www.sunstonewinery.com

ACCESS
From Highway 101, take Highway 246 exit and turn right. Go through Solvang and into Santa Ynez. Turn right on Refugio Road and go 2 miles. Winery is on right.

Hours for visits and tastings:
10AM – 4PM daily.
Closed on major holidays.

Wheelchair access.

TASTINGS & TOURS
Charge for tasting: $7; includes glass.

Free tours. Groups of ten or more by appointment only.

Typical wines offered: Viognier, Chardonnay, Sauvignon Blanc, Merlot, Syrah, Cabernet Franc, Cabernet Sauvignon, and blends such as Eros and Rapsodie du Soleil.

Wine-related items for sale.

PICNICS & PROGRAMS
Picnic area open to public. No picnic ingredients sold in tasting room. Pick up a picnic lunch at El Rancho Market or New Frontiers Natural Marketplace, both on Highway 246.

Special events: Valentine's Day dinner, Merlot for Mother's Day, Harvest Stomp party, Wild West BBQ, and other events. Check website for event calendar.

Wine club.

in his Santa Ynez tasting room, a recreation of Monet's studio in Giverny. His blends from different vineyards and vintages range from Bordeaux and Rhône to Italian varietals. The blending is done in an untraditional manner. Bion ferments half the wine himself at the Sunstone facility and augments the other half by purchasing barreled wine from another producer. He believes that winemaking is an art: "It's a lot like painting. An artist would never choose one color. You get a lot more opportunity to create depth, complexity, and balance through blending." The bottles are graced with fine-art labels on the front and the name of the wine and blend on the back. ☉☉

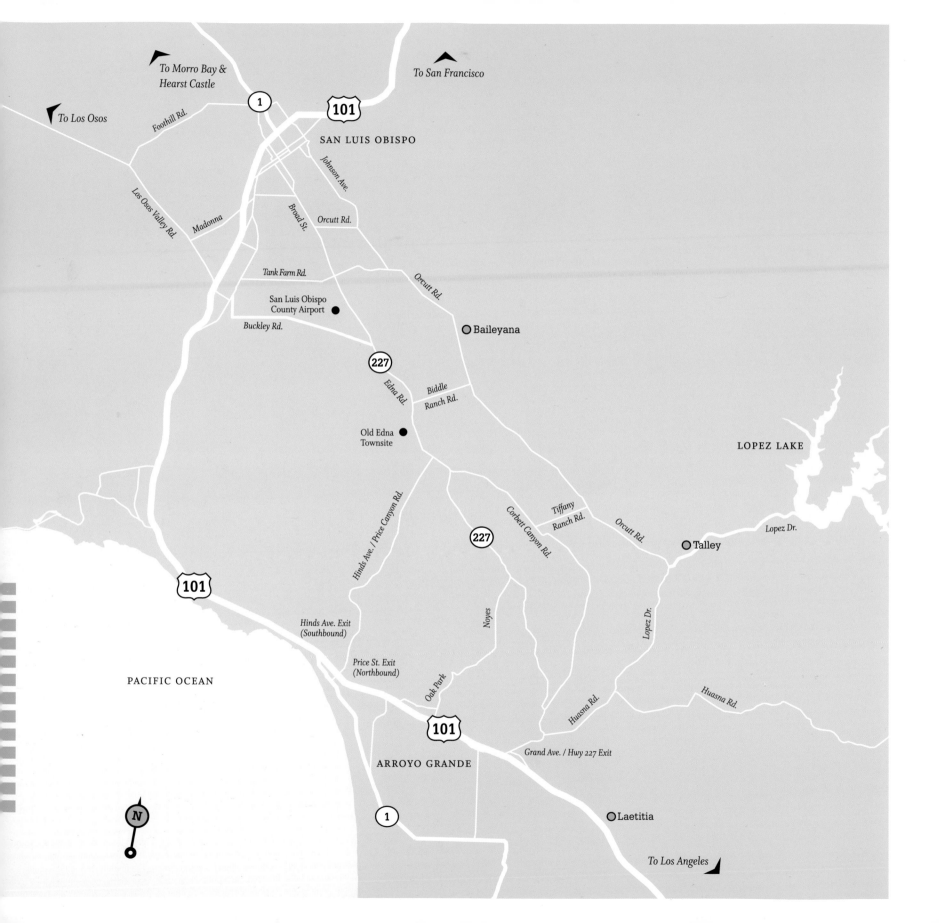

Arroyo Grande Valley & Edna Valley

THE WINERIES

Baileyana Winery

Laetitia Vineyard & Winery

Talley Vineyards

Baileyana Winery

The charm of Baileyana starts in its tasting room. Dating from 1909, the one-room Independence Schoolhouse operated for forty-seven years. After it closed in 1956, it was briefly used as a private residence, but then fell into disrepair. The Niven family rescued the historic treasure in 1996. After restoration was completed in 1998, the former schoolhouse opened its doors as Baileyana's tasting room. The building overlooks the expansive thousand acres of Niven family–owned Paragon Vineyards planted to Syrah, Chardonnay, Pinot Noir, and thirty-year-old vines of Sauvignon Blanc.

Although the yellow schoolhouse is almost a century old, Baileyana's history goes back only to the mid-1980s, when Catharine Niven, one of California's first female vintners, started the winery as a pet project. Originally from Kentucky, Catharine had a number of passionate interests: owning racehorses, collecting rare antiques, and sharing cooking tips with Julia Child. Then her husband John introduced her to California's wine region. The Nivens pioneered Edna Valley when they planted Paragon Vineyards in the early 1970s. At the time, the family wanted only to grow grapes. They later partnered with the Chalone Group, a collaboration that resulted in Edna Valley Winery. Recently, Diageo purchased Chalone, becoming the new co-owner of Edna Valley Winery. The Nivens retain full ownership of both Paragon and Firepeak Vineyards.

While Jack Niven was busy overseeing the family's large-scale grape growing, Catharine poured her energy into the three-and-a-half-acre parcel of vineyard in her front yard, creating Baileyana, named after the neighborhood in northern California where Catharine first met Jack. "She was the type of person that if she got into something, she jumped into it," fondly recalls grandson John H. Niven, Baileyana's director of sales and marketing. Catharine immersed herself in meticulous research, starting with the region of Burgundy. Although Edna Valley's conditions differ from those of Burgundy, she was determined to take the Burgundian approach to viticulture and wine making. Baileyana's first vintage was launched in 1991, with winemaker Gary Mosby as consultant, later succeeded by Bruno D'Alfonso. Christian Roguenant, a native of Dijon, France, came in 1998 and put his Burgundian stamp on Baileyana. As head enologist for the house of Maison Deutz, Roguenant had traveled to five continents to make wine. He didn't have to travel far when he left Laetitia in Arroyo Grande to join Baileyana a few miles north in Edna Valley.

Baileyana's state-of-the-art winery, located a quarter mile north of the tasting room, was built in 1999 to Roguenant's specifications. Large windows allow in filtered sunlight, not so much for the wines but to create a pleasant place for the staff and to save on energy costs. Roguenant's old-world winemaking techniques benefit from the high-tech facility. For example, each tank is controlled by a remote computer that warns the winemaker, via telephone, of any temperature fluctuations in the tank.

The winery sits atop a knoll, surrounded by Firepeak Vineyard, which forms the core of Baileyana's wine program. Planted in 1995, the vineyard's slopes are divided into forty-four blocks planted to a variety of clones: mutations or subdivisions of a varietal that play an important role in the viticulture of Pinot Noir, Chardonnay, and Syrah, each having a distinctive character. The vineyards benefit from the cool maritime influences and are located at the foot of Islay Mountain, the last in the chain of extinct volcanoes known as the Seven Sisters. The volcanic soil, called *diablo*, or "dirt of the devil," stresses the vines and intensifies their varietal character.

Baileyana's main program focuses on prized Firepeak Vineyard, which produces Grand Firepeak Cuvée Pinot Noir, rich with black raspberry fruit; Grand Firepeak Cuvée Chardonnay, a blend from the vineyard's different lots and rows; and berry-laced, spice-packed Grand Firepeak Cuvée Syrah. Baileyana's annual production of ten thousand to fifteen thousand cases includes Pinot Gris, port, and its signature Sauvignon Blanc. In 2005 Baileyana launched Tangent (meaning "deviation") to focus on a family of fresh whites such as Sauvignon Blanc, Pinot Gris, Pinot Blanc, Albarino, and Viognier, as well as Sauvignon Musque, part of the original Paragon planting. These whites are bottled both as single varietals and as a blend under the Halo label.

On a visit, you'll sample some blends available only through the tasting room. When creating these special wines, Roguenant welcomes advice from tasting-room staff for the final blend. Among the single varietals, be sure to try Baileyana's fragrant Syrah rosé and the dry Gewürztraminer, whose fragrance evokes a walk through a field of flowers. Ecclestone, a white table wine tracing its name to a small village in Scotland, is a refreshing blend that varies with each vintage but typically consists of Pinot Gris, Semillon, and Sauvignon Blanc. These wines and the crisp Tangent whites are a perfect match for seafood or for sipping on a summer afternoon while relaxing on the porch.

BAILEYANA WINERY // 5828 Orcutt Road, San Luis Obispo, CA 93401

T 805.269.8200
F 805.781.3635
E info@baileyana.com

www.baileyana.com

ACCESS
From downtown San Luis Obispo, take Broad Street south for 2.5 miles. Turn left at Tank Farm Road, which becomes Orcutt Road. Proceed for 4.5 miles. Winery is on left.

Hours for visits and tastings:
10AM–5PM daily.
Closed on major holidays.

Wheelchair access.

TASTINGS & TOURS
Charge for tasting: $5 for five to seven wines.

No tours.

Typical wines offered: Chardonnay, Pinot Noir, Syrah, Sauvignon Blanc, Pinot Gris, port, and sparkling wines.

Wine-related items for sale.

PICNICS & PROGRAMS
Picnic area open to public. No picnic ingredients sold in tasting room. Pick up a picnic lunch in Arroyo Grande.

No special events.

Wine club.

Laetitia Vineyard & Winery

OWNERS: SELIM ZILKHA & NADIA WELLISZ // WINEMAKER: ERIC HICKEY

Perched high above Highway 101, Laetitia offers a spectacular view of Arroyo Grande Valley. A winding flower-lined driveway leads to the parking lot, where a bocce ball court and an educational vineyard welcome you. As you make your way to the tasting room, you will notice rows of Pinot Noir vines marked with descriptions of different trellis systems. Take a few minutes to walk around this small vineyard. The professional staff or winemaker Eric Hickey will be happy to answer any questions. In the spacious tasting room, elaborate dried-flower arrangements in a dramatic copper vase and two vintage grape-picker baskets hang high above the tasting counter.

Originally the home of the French Champagne producer Maison Deutz, Laetitia is now owned by Selim Zilkha and his daughter, Nadia Wellisz. A native of Baghdad, Zilkha purchased the property in the 1990s, which allowed him to pursue his passion for farming. The vast eighteen-hundred-acre ranch is home to the winery, the tasting room, the Zilkha estate house, and a pet llama that can sometimes be seen wandering the grounds. Some four hundred acres, the majority of the vineyards, are planted to Pinot Noir, and the balance to Chardonnay and Pinot Blanc. With an abundant grape production, Laetitia sells its Pinot Noir fruit to wineries such as Tantara, Ambullneo, and Wild Horse.

Laetitia has a rounded portfolio of wines, ranging from Burgundy and Bordeaux to Rhône varietals, but is famed for its Pinot Noir. The vineyards are blessed with the cool ocean breezes and fog ideally suited for this grape. Other qualities that enhance the production of Laetitia's exceptional wines are the well-drained gravelly clay-loam soil and winemaker Eric Hickey's sustainable farming techniques. Detailed attention is paid to tending the vineyards. Goats and sheep help with weed abatement, and cover crops reduce soil erosion and increase biodiversity by attracting beneficial insects and microorganisms. The grape pomace—seeds, stems, pulp, and skins—is recycled and used to fertilize the vineyards. Nesting boxes for owls and woodland areas support predators such as red-tailed hawks and barn owls. An area for gardening is set aside for employees who commute from urban areas.

In addition to Laetitia's estate Pinot Noir, the winery's pride and joy are La Colline, an elegant wine with a touch of spice, and Les Galets. *Galets* means "pebbles" in French, and the vineyard is named for the porous stone found on the site. Located on a hillside adjacent to the tasting room, these vineyards produce limited quantities of exceptional Pinot Noir.

Laetitia continues the Maison Deutz tradition of making sparkling wine in the *méthode champenoise* style, which originated in France's Champagne region. The wines are crafted by Eric's father, David Hickey, the winemaker for sparkling wines since the start of Maison Deutz. At Laetitia, some sparkling wines are made from 100 percent Pinot Noir or 100 percent Chardonnay and others from a combination of the two grapes with some Pinot Blanc. At harvest time, from mid-August to mid-September, visitors can see David Hickey operating the two ten-foot-round Coquard basket presses, the only ones existing in the United States. An additional tasting counter is set up as a viewing area, and on occasion Hickey will hand samples of grape juice to visitors for a taste. Laetitia's annual production of sparkling wine totals three thousand cases. Other wineries might make a few hundred cases or so, but Laetitia is seriously dedicated to sparkling-wine production.

While Laetitia is near the coast, its sister winery, Barnwood, is at an elevation of three thousand feet on Cuyama Peak in the Sierra Madre Mountains. Zilkha is introducing Bordeaux, Rhône, and Spanish varietals to the region. His seven hundred acres of plantings on the nineteen-hundred-acre property constitute the only large vineyard in the area. The rugged terrain and high elevation, coupled with the exposure to sunlight, guarantee the grapes' fully ripe character, resulting in Barnwood's bold and daring signature wines. The wines are appropriately named. The Grenache is called Rocky Road, the Tempranillo is dubbed Untamed, and the Cabernet goes by 3200, after the elevation of its vineyard. Barnwood is not open to the public, but you can taste the wines at Laetitia.

The scenic grounds at Laetitia are spectacular throughout the year. In springtime, the gardens are abloom. In fall, as the leaves turn color, the vineyards become a rich tapestry of flaming reds and burnished golds. The months of September and October, when the fog recedes, are surprisingly warm. Whatever season you visit, you'll always find a cool ocean breeze. Be sure to stroll down to La Colline Vineyard, where you can enjoy a picnic on the patio and celebrate with a glass of bubbly. ⋙

LAETITIA VINEYARD & WINERY // 453 Laetitia Vineyard Drive, Arroyo Grande, CA 93420

T 888.809.VINE; 805.481.1772
F 805.481.6920
E info@laetitiawine.com

www.laetitiawine.com

ACCESS

Located between Santa Maria and San Luis Obispo, 5 miles north of Nipomo. Winery's driveway is on the east side, directly off Highway 101. Two flags (United States and California) marking entrance are visible from a distance.

Hours for visits and tastings:
11AM–5PM daily.
Closed on major holidays.

Wheelchair access.

TASTINGS & TOURS

Charge only for reserve tasting.

No tours.

Typical wines offered: Pinot Noir, Chardonnay, Pinot Blanc, and sparkling wines from Laetitia. Cabernet Sauvignon, Sauvignon Blanc, Trio (red blend), Petite Sirah, and Tempranillo from Barnwood.

Wine-related items for sale.

PICNICS & PROGRAMS

Picnic area open to public. Picnic ingredients sold in tasting room.

Special events: Harvest Festival and Roll Out the Barrels. Check website for event calendar.

Wine club.

Few tasting rooms allow you to sample wines and also to pick up fresh produce. On entering the Talley Vineyards tasting room, you'll find baskets brimming with seasonal vegetables, such as heirloom tomatoes, peppers, cucumbers, and avocados. At grape-harvest time, they will be filled with a variety of squashes and pumpkins. As you savor Talley's crisp Chardonnays and velvety Pinot Noirs, you'll be enchanted not only by the sweeping view of the vines but also by the expansive vegetable farm below the hillside vineyards.

Long before planting vineyards, the Talley family was known for its farms. Oliver Talley started planting specialty vegetables in 1948 in the Arroyo Grande Valley. A total of fifteen hundred acres are now planted to row crops, and the tradition of farming and winemaking continues with the family's second and third generations. Because of the valley's northeast-southwest orientation, the Talley ranch benefits from cool Pacific Ocean breezes, a climate regarded as ideal for grape growing. Oliver's son, Don, recognized this potential in the hillsides above the vegetable farm. After research and analysis, he planted a small area in 1982 that gradually expanded to the current two hundred acres. Talley produced its first wine in 1986 with a mere 450 cases. The annual production now ranges between 12,000 and 14,000 cases. From a small production area located near one of the vegetable warehouses, the facility expanded to the current eighty-five-hundred-square-foot winery and tasting room, completed in 1991 at the foot of Talley's Rincon Vineyard.

The first landmark you see as you approach Talley's estate is El Rincon Adobe, which is depicted on Talley's label. Dating to 1860, the building changed hands several times until the Talley family purchased the property in 1974. It was restored in 1988 and served as the tasting room. Before then, the adobe was the oldest continuously inhabited residence in San Luis Obispo County. It now holds the winery's administrative office and also serves as a venue for special events.

Talley is renowned for its four exceptional vineyards, including Rincon Vineyard (whose fruit is sourced by Au Bon Climat) and Rosemary's Vineyard in Arroyo Grande Valley. The other two are in neighboring Edna Valley: Oliver's Vineyard, planted exclusively to Chardonnay, and Stone Corral, a twenty-eight-acre Pinot Noir vineyard. Eighty-seven-acre Rincon, Talley's oldest vineyard, was planted in 1982 and named after the historic adobe. Most of the acreage is devoted to Chardonnay and Pinot Noir, with the balance to Syrah, Semillon, Cabernet Franc, Sauvignon Blanc, and Riesling. The shallow soil, combined with steep hillsides, encourages good drainage and produces a small yield.

Located a mile west of Rincon, Rosemary's Vineyard is also on a steep hillside and surrounds Don and Rosemary Talley's home. Plantings of Chardonnay and Pinot Noir on the twenty-eight-acre vineyard were started in 1987 and completed in 2001. The top 7 percent of fruit from Rosemary's and Rincon vineyards is bottled as its prized vineyard-designated Pinot Noir and Chardonnay. The Rincon Pinot Noir is redolent of black fruits accented with black pepper, while the one from Rosemary's shows aromas of raspberry with a hint of cloves. The remaining fruit from both vineyards is blended as the winery's signature vanilla-laced Estate Chardonnay and a spicy and vibrant Estate Pinot Noir. Talley also makes a zesty Estate Sauvignon Blanc blended with 25 percent Semillon.

Third-generation Brian Talley, the winery's president, works closely with consulting winemaker Steve Rasmussen, production manager Victor Cuevos, and enologist Leslie Mead. The team practices organic farming in certain parts of the vineyards. Cover crops are planted in the vineyards to prevent erosion and improve soil conditions. Organic compost is produced from a combination of horse manure and grape pomace (skin, seeds, stems, and pulp). Talley's highly trained team does much of the work by hand and is quick to report anything out of the ordinary in the vineyard. "Since they literally touch each vine five times during the course of the season, they are very much the eyes and ears of the vineyard," notes Brian Talley.

The Talley family produces a second tier of wines under the Bishop's Peak label, named for the ancient

---

76

TALLEY VINEYARDS // 3031 Lopez Drive, Arroyo Grande, CA 93402

T 805.489.0446
F 805.489.0996
E info@talleyvineyards.com

www.talleyvineyards.com

ACCESS
From Highway 101, take Grand Avenue exit in Arroyo Grande and go east through Arroyo Grande. At three-way stop sign, keep to right and follow signs to Lopez Lake for 5.5 miles. Winery is on left.

Hours for visits and tastings:
10:30AM–4:30PM daily.
Closed on major holidays.

Wheelchair access.

TASTINGS & TOURS
Charge for tasting: $4 for five wines.

No tours.

Typical wines offered: Chardonnay, Pinot Noir, Sauvignon Blanc, Riesling, Cabernet Sauvignon, and Syrah.

Wine-related items for sale.

PICNICS & PROGRAMS
Picnic area open to public. Picnic ingredients sold in tasting room.

Special events: San Luis Obispo County Vintners' Association open house. Check website for event calendar.

Wine club.

volcano that towers above the city of San Luis Obispo. Producing between twelve thousand and fourteen thousand cases annually, the Talleys call this wine their "grower's label," as fruit is sourced from other growers. Brian Talley and winemaker Rasmussen work closely with the growers to ensure high-quality fruit. The Pinot Noir is from Avila Valley and Arroyo Grande Valley fruit, and the Syrah and Chardonnay are from Edna Valley. From Paso Robles' warm climate comes Cabernet Sauvignon and Rock Solid Red, a blend of Bordeaux and Rhône varietals. In 2005, the Talleys acquired the forty-acre Hazel Talley Vineyard in Paso, planted to Cabernet Sauvignon, Cabernet Franc, and Syrah. The Hazel Talley vineyard-designated wines will be bottled under the Bishop's Peak label and released in 2007.

Talley's grounds are beautifully landscaped with masses of lavender and rosemary mixed with daisies and roses. Picnic tables under patio umbrellas surround a fountain that anchors the entrance to the tasting room. An additional picnic area is set up in front of the adobe. The hilltop is a perfect spot to take in the vast, thriving farm that has been supplying vegetables for more than sixty years. ◡◡

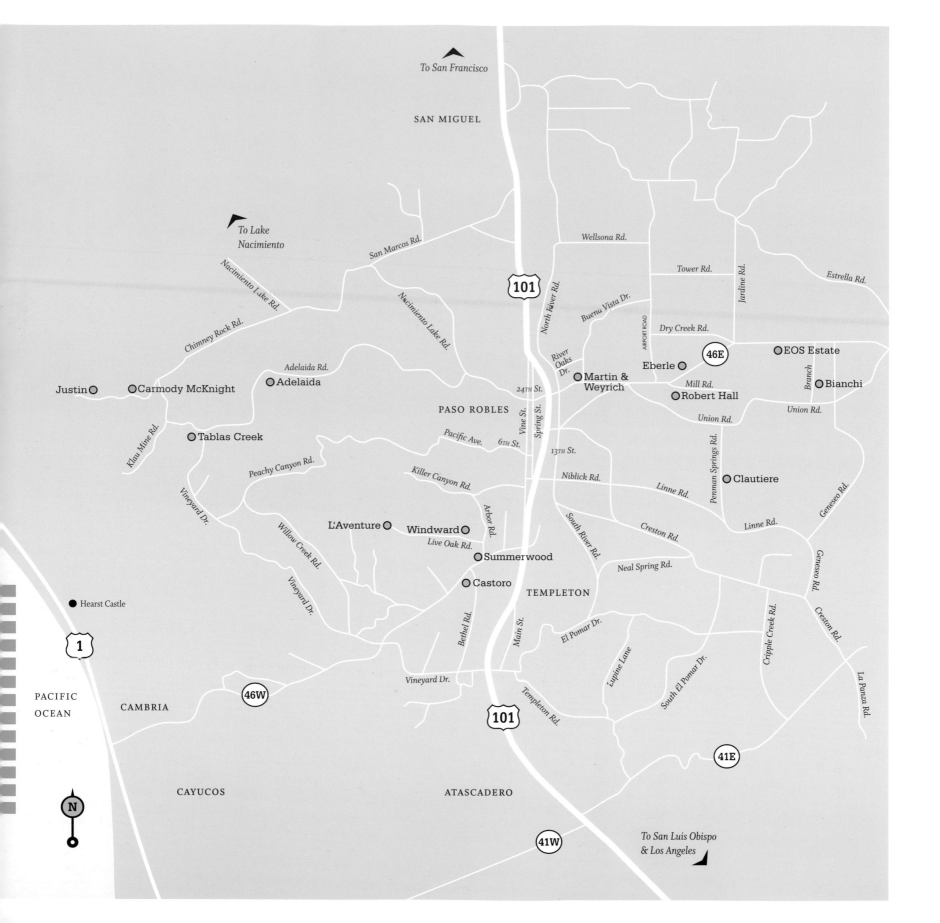

SAN LUIS OBISPO COUNTY NORTH

Paso Robles

THE WINERIES

- Adelaida Cellars
- Bianchi
- Carmody McKnight Estate Wines
- Castoro Cellars
- Clautiere Vineyard
- Eberle Winery
- EOS Estate Winery
- Justin Vineyards & Winery
- L'Aventure Winery
- Martin & Weyrich Winery
- Robert Hall Winery
- Summerwood Winery
- Tablas Creek Vineyard
- Windward Vineyard

Lush with manzanitas, oaks, and madrones, the scenic tree-shaded Adelaida Road winds past wineries on hillsides and up canyons. In the 1870s, the Adelaida region–an imprecisely defined area on Paso's west side –was inhabited by Mennonite dairy farmers. Earlier, the area played a historic role in providing a route for the Catalan *escolte*: soldiers who guarded the Franciscan missions between the Salinas Valley and the coast.

Adelaida Cellars is named after a nineteenth-century settlement in the Santa Lucia Mountains, and lies sixteen miles from the ocean, near the south end of the mountain range. The winery is noted for its mountain-grown wines. It's not only one of the Far Out Wineries, it is also sky high, as its vineyards are planted on steep slopes at an elevation of two thousand feet. The entire vineyard property lies to the southeast of the winery, less than a mile away, and spans three ranches that are almost contiguous. A panoramic view of the rugged mountaintop property looks like a giant jigsaw puzzle, with large blocks of well-manicured vineyards interrupted by walnut and almond groves. Due to the high elevation, the vineyards get the best sun exposure as well as the cool breezes that blow through the break in the coastal region known as the Templeton Gap. A marine layer helps develop fruit acidity and ripeness. This cool climate makes this area prime Pinot Noir and Chardonnay country. Thus, Adelaida Cellars' Pinot Noir is a riot of succulent cherries and earthy elements, the Chardonnay is flinty with hints of lemon zest, and the silky smooth Syrah is redolent with black cherry aromas. What makes the wine special at Adelaida Cellars, besides the elevation, is the chalky limestone soil, a rarity in California, explains winemaker Terry Culton. The hillside vineyards benefit from the shallow limestone soils, as the vine roots are stressed and push through the rocky soil for nutrients. This controls vine vigor, resulting in low yields and producing a concentrated, intense flavor in the fruit.

The Adelaida Cellars label was established in 1981 by noted winemaker John Munch, current owner of Le Cuvier Winery. Munch had no vineyards of his own, so he purchased grapes and made his wines at different facilities. He became acquainted with his neighbors Don and Elizabeth Van Steenwyk, who had purchased a large ranch with walnut and almond groves as an investment in the 1970s. Charmed by Munch, the Van Steenwyks formed an alliance with him and built a winery on their ranch in 1991. Munch was the winemaker. The partnership dissolved in 1998, with the Van Steenwyks retaining both the property and the name. Elizabeth minds the winery as general manager, while Don looks after his electronics business.

In 1994, the Van Steenwyks purchased part of the historic Hoffman Mountain Ranch Estate (HMR) from a Japanese conglomerate. These famed vineyards were originally planted in 1963 by Beverly Hills cardiologist Stanley Hoffman, the pioneer who planted Cabernet Sauvignon, Chardonnay, and the first Pinot Noir in the region. The Van Steenwyks rejuvenated the HMR vineyards, which were then in total disrepair. In addition to purchasing the HMR vineyards, the Van Steenwyks planted the Viking Estate Vineyard on the warmer side of the hillsides to grow Cabernet Sauvignon and Syrah grapes. Five acres of Mourvèdre and Grenache are planted high above the Syrah, and will be blended with this varietal for its Rhône Cuvée.

Adelaida wines are bottled in four labels. The reserve label is exclusively for "barrel select" wine. Culton may select the very best grapes for the reserve when the fruit arrives for crushing, or he might wait to see how the wine matures in the barrels and designate the wine for the reserve label at that stage. The Adelaida label gets the best non-reserve wine; the SLO label (signifying San Luis Obispo County) is bottled with grapes not used for the Adelaida label; and the affordable Schoolhouse label is for non-estate grapes. The total annual production is around fifteen thousand cases, which include both red and white Rhône blends, Pinot Noir, Zinfandel, Cabernet Sauvignon, Chardonnay, and the signature Syrah, loaded with intense blackberry fruit. The winery also produces small quantities of Pinot Noir rosé, Sangiovese, and Barbera.

A walnut orchard and the Bobcat Crossing Vineyards, named after a family of bobcats inhabiting

ADELAIDA CELLARS // 5805 Adelaida Road, Paso Robles, CA 93446

T 805.239.8980
F 805.239.4671
E info@adelaida.com

www.adelaida.com

ACCESS
From Highway 101, take 24th Street exit in Paso Robles. Follow 24th west until it turns into Nacimiento Lake Drive. Go 1 mile and turn left on Adelaida Road. Continue for 5.3 miles. Winery is on left.

Hours for visits and tastings:
11AM– 5PM daily.
Closed on major holidays.

Wheelchair access.

TASTINGS & TOURS
Charge for tastings: $4 for six or seven wines, including regular glass; $10 includes Spiegelau crystal glass.

Tours by appointment only.

Typical wines offered: Pinot Noir, Cabernet Sauvignon, Zinfandel, and Rhône varietals.

Wine-related items for sale.

PICNICS & PROGRAMS
Picnic area open to public. No picnic ingredients sold in tasting room.

Special events: Paso Robles Wine Festival, third weekend of May; Harvest Wine Tour, third weekend of October.

Wine club.

the property, flank the quarter-mile scenic drive leading up to the winery. Inside an intimate tasting room, you have a view of the fermentation room holding large stainless-steel tanks. An oak-topped bar counter is lined with tasting bottles and bowls of Adelaida almonds, accompanied with a stack of recipes for making the snack. This is, of course, designed to tempt purchases of sacks of organic almonds and walnuts fresh from the orchard. Other merchandise includes beautifully fashioned cutting boards made from oak barrel remnants handcrafted by Larry Golden. The Arizona artist also designed the doors to the tasting room and fermentation room, which are fashioned from the discarded oak uprights of large storage barrels.

There are no official tours of the vineyards, but depending on your level of interest and staff availability, the winery will oblige with the one-hour tour of the steep hillside vineyards. "We are very proud of our vineyards, but they are not easy to get to," says Elizabeth Van Steenwyk. Conducted in a four-wheel-drive truck by Culton or Paul Sowerby, the winery's national sales manager, the tour is one bumpy but breathtaking ride. Driving along spectacular slopes, you will make brief stops at certain vista points and learn about the various vineyards. From one of the hilltops, you can take in the vast panorama of the Adelaida region with the town of Paso in the distance. The winery is noted for educational seminars, such as the annual Zinfandel Summit that brings together a group of winemakers of the Far Out Wineries, and events such as the popular Mother's Day Brunch and monthly summer barbecues held on the mountainside terrace with its sweeping view of Adelaida Hills. ⋏

Bianchi

OWNER: **GLENN BIANCHI** // WINEMAKER: **TOM LANE**

Tranquility pervades Bianchi. The soothing sound of a waterfall envelops the property. The yellow building that houses the tasting room seems to rise from a serene lake shaded by a Modesto ash tree. A terrace on the lake's edge holds umbrella-topped tables and chairs. A classic old oak towers over the red-tinted guest house across from the tasting room, and behind the house stands a large green building that houses the winery. Surrounding this Zen-like ambience are acres of Merlot, Cabernet Sauvignon, Syrah, and Zinfandel vineyards.

The winery's building, designed by the San Luis Obispo firm of Steven Pults & Associates, is a graceful combination of cultured stone and floor-to-ceiling glass walls that bring the exterior beauty of the vineyards inside the tasting room. Owner Glenn Bianchi originally conceived a mission-style structure, but couldn't be happier with the results: an ultra-modern barn with high ceilings. "To most people it looks like a barn," he says, "but to me it feels like a church or a chapel with lofty ceilings." In charge of the winery's design, Tim Mark Woodle, AIA, the firm's partner, defines it as a contemporary approach to Bianchi's mission style concept. Stone plays an important role in the design, as it represents the essence of the wine business. "Stone is permanent and is an expression of the permanence of the industry," comments Woodle.

The Bianchi family has been making wine for three decades. Under the label of Villa Bianchi, they initially produced generic wines, such as Chablis, rosé, and Chianti in Kerman, California. In 2000, Glenn Bianchi chose Paso Robles as the location for making the transition to ultra-premium wines. The forty-acre property he purchased on Branch Road included vineyards, a house, and an old metal shed that was remodeled into a state-of-the-art winery. The former irrigation pond was reshaped into a lake, which is popular with visitors. The winery and the tasting room were completed in 2004 with the first harvest. The thirty-two acres of vineyards produce fifteen thousand to eighteen thousand cases annually.

Winemaker Tom Lane's approach is all about "layers." Together, he says, they add up to more than the sum of their parts. Lane's first layer starts in the vineyard just before harvest time. To ensure perfect ripeness, he spends a good part of each day tasting a random sampling of grapes before he permits them to be picked. Lane's second layer occurs in the winery, where he works with various types of yeasts that contribute to different flavors and tannin profiles. He keenly monitors the length of fermentation, which determines the subtle nuances of the wine. When it comes to barrel selection, Lane uses both American and French oak, some new and others four to five years old. Depending on the type of wine, Lane will select medium- to heavy-toasted barrels. All new barrels are toasted, or charred, on the inside over an open flame. This caramelizes the wood and imparts a vanilla character to the wine.

The final blending, the winemaker's third layer, could entail blending different varietals or a single varietal from different vineyards. Lane also blends a single varietal that's been aged in different barrels. The type of wood and the way the barrel was toasted add different nuances to the wine. The result is a lineup of well-balanced wines, such as Cabernet Sauvignon, Merlot, Syrah, and Zinfandel, made with estate fruit under the Heritage Collection label. The Signature Collection includes a crisp Chardonnay with fruit from Edna Valley and a seductive Pinot Noir from York Mountain appellation. The Pinot Grigio is bottled with fruit from Arroyo Grande, and the Petite Sirah and Cabernet Franc from different vineyards in Paso Robles. Lane is also building an Italian theme with bottlings of Sangiovese and Barbera and a small production of Refosco, a late-ripening grape that is ideal with pasta. The fruit for Italian varietals is purchased from different vineyards in Paso Robles.

An uplifting mood permeates the tasting room, as light filters in through the glass doors and windows. The interior's design layout is an artistic assemblage of materials: wood, stone, steel, polished concrete and glass. The curved wall behind the tasting counter serves as a division between the back office and the front tasting area. The concrete tasting counter is accented by sandblasted glass and raw steel. The room is stacked with beautiful gift items, from fine hand-crafted jewelry to Italian ceramics. Tapestry pillows by the fireplace invite you to relax. Fleece blankets are supplied on chilly days. A deli case is well stocked with cold cuts and cheeses, and a humidor cradles fine cigars. A collection of remote-controlled sailboats will catch your eye. You are encouraged to have fun with these on the lake between tastings. The terrace jutting onto the lake makes a lovely picnic spot. For Bianchi's special events, the terrace serves as a stage for performers and musical groups.

Although the winery does not have official tours, Glenn Bianchi notes that his staff is very accommodating. Depending on your level of interest and the availability of the staff, you might be given a barrel tasting or get an inside look at the winery.

BIANCHI // 3380 Branch Road, Paso Robles, CA 93446

T 805.226.9922
F 805.226.8230
E info@bianchiwine.com

www.bianchiwine.com

ACCESS
From Highway 101, exit at Highway 46 East and go about 7 miles to Branch Road, then turn right. Winery is a short distance on left.

Hours for visits and tastings:
10AM – 5PM daily.
Closed on major holidays.

Wheelchair access.

TASTINGS & TOURS
Charge for tasting: first five wines complimentary; after that, $2 tasting fee.

No tours.

Typical wines offered: Pinot Noir, Pinot Grigio, Sauvignon Blanc, Chardonnay, Zinfandel, Merlot, Cabernet Sauvignon, Sangiovese, Refosco, Syrah, and Petite Sirah.

Wine-related items for sale.

PICNICS & PROGRAMS
Picnic area open to public. Picnic ingredients sold in tasting room.

Special events: Check website for event calendar.

Wine club.

How Gary and Marian McKnight Conway came to own this idyllic property on Paso's west side is a story made for celluloid. Conway (born Carmody), star of the popular television series *Land of the Giants* and *Burke's Law*, was looking for a weekend getaway when a fellow actor suggested Paso Robles. He surveyed the area with a real estate agent from a helicopter that crashed on a hilltop. "I walked away without a scratch and bought the property on the spot," Conway recalls. This was more than thirty years ago. Conway and his wife, Marian McKnight, a former Miss America, decided to make this fortunate spot their home "just to admire nature's beauty."

The previous owner mentioned that there was something special about this land, and for Conway, that something special was how the light filled the sky. The actor-turned-vintner has been a painter nearly his entire life. Deeply aware of the natural beauty around him, he especially admired the pristine blueness of the sky contrasted against the various shades of the green hills. However, one February morning in 2006, Conway was surprised to see his property covered under a stunning blanket of snow. He grabbed his camera and rushed out in his slippers and pajamas to capture this once-in-a-decade phenomenon. The snow melted in a few hours, and by the time the tasting room was opened, there were no signs of this divine intervention that occurred amidst the rugged Santa Lucia Mountains. Conway continues to capture the beauty of the landscape in oil paintings and photographs, both of which are displayed in the 150-year-old farmhouse that serves as Carmody McKnight's tasting room. For each vintage, Conway creates a new artwork for the labels, which has resulted in a substantial collection of his art.

The unique feature of the 160-acre property is a serene lake shaded by a weeping willow. An old oak that fell into the lake was left untouched as a natural sculpture. Seated by the water, you take in native oaks, black locust trees, five different types of pines, and rows of well-manicured Merlot and Cabernet Sauvignon vines hugging the hillsides. In the midst of this landscape is a grove of Tuscan olive trees. Oil is produced from the harvested olives at nearby Willow Creek Ranch and is sold in Carmody McKnight's tasting room.

Conway first tried his hand at growing barley and wheat but wasn't successful. He then learned that the soil was well suited for vineyards and plunged into viticulture education. The Conways planted their first vineyards in 1985. The first vintage was produced ten years later in the farmhouse cellar. The vintner soon discovered the special qualities of the ranch's soil, actually four different soils: calcareous shale, limestone, volcanic rocks, and montmorillonite, rare in California but found in abundance in the Carmody McKnight vineyards. So unusual is this combination that it has become the subject of extensive study and research by San Luis Obispo's California Polytechnic State University, assisted by companies such as John Deere Global Agricultural Services, Earth Information Technologies, and Motorola.

These special conditions allow Bordeaux varietals to thrive side by side with Burgundy, yielding some six thousand cases annually. Winemaker Greg Cropper produces three Chardonnays: Free-Run and Day in the Country, bright, crisp wines made from the juice released prior to the pressing of the fruit, and Marian's Vineyard Chardonnay, exuding aromas of pears and melon with just a hint of oak. The Pinot Noir is laced with blackberry flavors, while the deep garnet Cabernet Franc displays layers of cranberries and rose petals. A ruby red Cabernet Sauvignon releases aromas of cherries and cassis. Carmody McKnight also produces Cadenza, a popular Bordeaux blend;

a limited supply of sparkling wines; Late Harvest Cabernet Franc, a rare dessert wine made from this varietal; and a full-bodied port-style Merlot dessert wine.

One of the highlights of Carmody McKnight is the straw-bale barrel storage facility that functions like an above-ground cave. Made of rice straw and covered with plaster, the thick walls maintain a constant temperature around fifty-five degrees Fahrenheit. The twenty-five-hundred-square-foot building was designed by Semmes and Company, an Atascadero-based firm specializing in alternative energy and sustainable architecture.

When you visit Carmody McKnight, you will notice that there's a lot more going on than winemaking. The ranch has an organic garden and an animal farm with exotic chickens, doves, homing pigeons, horses, and Australian alpaca sheep. The wool from the sheep is knitted into sweaters by McKnight and friends for personal use.

The couple's daughter, Kathleen, uses the fresh organic produce to create healthy lunches on weekends. If you wish to picnic on the grounds, you can call ahead for a box lunch. To work off the meal, enjoy a pleasant hike along the vineyards perched at an elevation of sixteen hundred feet, and explore this lucky spot where Gary Conway found a new life. ❧

CARMODY McKNIGHT ESTATE WINES // 11240 Chimney Rock Road, Paso Robles, CA 93446

T 805.238.0302
F 805.238.3975
E info@carmodymcknight.com

www.carmodymcknight.com

ACCESS
From Highway 101, exit at Spring Street in Paso Robles. Continue to 24th Street, turn left, and go 17 miles to winery (24th Street turns into G14, also named Nacimiento Lake Road, leading to Chimney Rock Road)

Hours for visits and tastings:
10AM – 5PM daily.
Closed on major holidays.

Wheelchair access.

TASTINGS & TOURS
Charge for tastings: $5 for seven or eight wines; includes logo glass.

Tours by appointment only.

Typical wines offered: Chardonnay, Pinot Noir, Cabernet Franc, Merlot, Cabernet Sauvignon, Bordeaux-style blends, dessert wines, late-harvest wines, and sparkling wines.

Wine-related items for sale.

PICNICS & PROGRAMS
Picnic area open to public. No picnic ingredients sold in tasting room. Call ahead for a picnic lunch prepared by Kathleen Conway.

Special events: Lakeside lunches and winemaker dinners. Check website for event calendar.

Wine club.

Castoro Cellars

OWNERS: NIELS & BIMMER UDSEN // WINEMAKER: TOM MYERS

Castoro Cellars' beaver mascot may seem like an odd choice for a winery. But there's a story behind it. Owners Niels and Bimmer Udsen are originally from Denmark, where Niels goes by the nickname "Beaver." So they named the winery Castoro, Italian for "beaver." The label sports an image of a beaver nibbling on a cluster of grapes. Below it is a line that reads "Dam Fine Wine," in reference to beaver dams. "We don't take ourselves too seriously," says Bimmer Udsen.

While they may take themselves lightheartedly, the Udsens approach their wines seriously. Their blends are impressive, reflecting the character of Paso's fruit, which is ready to drink when young but worthy of cellaring for a few years. Castoro Cellars is among the handful of wineries that pioneered Paso's proprietary blend: a bold combination of Bordeaux and Rhône varietals. Dubbed "Super Paso" – similar to Super Tuscan, a blend of the Italian Sangiovese grape and Bordeaux varietals like Merlot and Cabernet Sauvignon–the Paso blend can also include Zinfandel. The blending concept started in the mid-1990s, when the couple decided that they could combine different varietals depending on what Mother Nature provided. The free-spirited husband-and-wife team decided to buck the trend of creating a typical Bordeaux-style wine: of Cabernet Sauvignon, Merlot, and Cabernet Franc. Not to be bound by restrictions, the team embarked on blending Bordeaux and Rhône varietals. But they felt the blend had to include Zinfandel, a grape so popular in this region that it commands its own annual festival in March. The result was Diciannove Anni, a blend of Cabernet Sauvignon, Cabernet Franc, Petite Sirah, and Zinfandel. Launched in 1991, the cult wine's combination and percentage of varietals varies each year depending on the season's harvest. But it will always include a touch of Zin.

Although Niels and Bimmer grew up enjoying wine as an essential part of a meal, it wasn't until Niels spent a year in Italy after high school that he developed a taste for wine. After studying agricultural business management at California Polytechnic State University, San Luis Obispo, he took a marketing job at Zaca Mesa Winery. In 1981, the Udsens moved to Paso, and Niels worked as a "cellar rat" at Estrella River Winery (now Meridian Vineyards and Winery) with Tom Meyers, who now heads Castoro's wine-making team. While Niels was at Estrella, the Udsens started making their own wine on the side in a trash can. "We didn't have any capital," Niels recalls, "so we sold wine to make more wine." They continued to do just that for five years. Niels helped set up the J. Lohr Winery and continued to make his wines there. Finally, in 1991, the Udsens purchased their own winery off the beaten path in San Miguel. The following year, the elaborate tasting room opened at the corner of Highway 46 West and Bethel Road in Templeton.

Castoro is recognized for its long list of highly affordable wines. Its signature wines are Zinfandel, from the estate's Giubbini and Cobble Creek vineyards, and Zinfusion, a wine blended from three different vineyards and complemented with a splash of Petite Sirah. The Udsens also purchase fruit from more than twenty growers in the Paso area. Castoro's production facility is so spacious that it handles the crush for prestigious wineries that buy fruit from the area, labels such as Hess Select, Fetzer, Stags' Leap, Maddalena, Mondavi's Coastal, and the former Niebaum-Coppola, now renamed Rubicon Estate.

A hundred-foot-long arbor of Zinfandel grapes creates a scenic entryway to Castoro's Mediterranean-style tasting room. Masses of lavender flank the pathway, and grape arbors abound in the garden area. At harvest time, the arbors are lush with plump, juicy Zinfandel grapes within easy reach for plucking. The beautifully landscaped courtyard meanders around pathways to out-of-the-way corners that make ideal picnic spots. A spacious art gallery exhibiting local artists is adjacent to the tasting room, and a shady Zinfandel arbor overlooks the sprawling Cobble Creek Vineyards.

This picture-perfect setting is popular with visitors. The tasting room can get five deep at times, but an adjoining room is always ready to accommodate the spillover. The tasting lineup, including more than a dozen wines, starts with Pinot Blanc, Viognier, and Chardonnay, then proceeds to Syrah, Merlot, Cabernet Sauvignon, Pinot Noir, Petit Verdot, Zinfandel, and Primitivo, and ends with a late-harvest Muscat Canelli. You can spend as much time wine tasting as browsing around the room, which has an impressive collection of gifts and gourmet foods. Castoro stages a keen program of summer concerts in the amphitheater, so do check the website for the event calendar. A visit to Castoro is a special treat at any season – but especially at harvest time, when you can picnic under the cool shade of the grape arbor and reach out for a bunch of luscious Zinfandel grapes.

CASTORO CELLARS // 1315 North Bethel Road, Templeton, CA 93465

T 888.DAM.FINE
F 805.238.2602
E info@castorocellars.com

www.castorocellars.com

ACCESS
From Highway 101, exit at Highway 46 West. Go west for 1.2 miles and turn left on Bethel Road. Winery is on right.

Hours for visits and tastings:
10AM–5:30PM daily.
Closed major holidays.

Wheelchair access.

TASTINGS & TOURS
Charge for tasting: Three wines complimentary; $3 for seven wines, including logo glass; seven tastes free with wine purchase.

No tours.

Typical wines offered: Chardonnay, Fumé Blanc, Viognier, Pinot Blanc, Cabernet Sauvignon, Zinfandel (single varietals and blends), Pinot Noir, Merlot, Tempranillo, Syrah, Bordeaux-style blends and proprietary blends, late-harvest Zinfandel, and Muscat Canelli.

Wine-related items for sale.

PICNICS & PROGRAMS
Picnic area open to public. Picnic ingredients sold in the tasting room.

Special events: Concerts, art openings, and winemaker dinners. Check website for calendar.

Wine club.

Clautiere Vineyard

OWNERS: **CLAUDINE BLACKWELL & TERRY BRADY** // WINEMAKER: **TERRY BRADY**

If you're planning to visit Clautiere Vineyard, be prepared to leave your inhibitions at the gate. It's an eye-popping experience best described as "Edward Scissorhands meets the Mad Hatter at the Moulin Rouge." Owners Claudine Blackwell and Terry Brady have taken the snobbery out of wine tasting and injected it with a good dose of whimsy. From the grounds to the tasting room, they've created a truly enchanting winery. A handcrafted curlicue steel fence encircles the property, which is landscaped with elegant, tall tufts of forty varieties of grass. As you wander the grounds, you'll encounter magnificent metal sculptures, and fences fashioned from used vine stakes. In the center of this magical landscape is a red-tinted Craftsman-style house with a wraparound deck. Gaudíesque mosaic pillars stand guard at the tasting-room entrance, where a gold-flecked door welcomes you to an interior as vibrant as the Clautiere varietals are bold.

Inside the colorfully appointed front room, baskets of wild-colored wigs and eccentric hats are stacked by the fireplace. You'll be encouraged to wear one of these headpieces as you embark on your wine-tasting journey. If it so happens that the day of your visit is your birthday, the wig you are wearing will be crowned with a diamond tiara, and you'll be photographed for posterity. The festive atmosphere extends to all patrons. Every time a wine club member enters the room or a new member joins the club, a large brass gong is struck as the crowd joins in with a loud cheer.

Claudine Blackwell, who carries the title "director of fantasy," constructed the 230-foot fence and the sculptures. From designing lingerie and hatboxes to welding sculptures, Blackwell has long been an artist. Her husband, Terry Brady, makes the wine. Their exuberant personalities and their motto, "live the best life you can live," are reflected in the winery's logo of a diamond harlequin design accented with stripes. Which is not to say they are frivolous about their wines. The Blackwell-Brady team is committed to producing small, exceptional lots of handcrafted Rhône varietals. During the year, they lovingly tend their vineyards and, come harvest time, are busy driving forklifts, moving bins, punching down grapes, and putting passion into wine production. Their creativity stretches from the exterior landscape and whimsical tasting room to what's captured in the bottle.

Former Los Angeles residents, Brady and Blackwell wanted to embark on an out-of-town project in 1999, perhaps growing trees. Their real estate agent suggested looking at vineyards in Paso. "We didn't even know there were vineyards in Paso," exclaims Blackwell. It took them six days to leave raising trees behind and to finalize the vineyard purchase. They settled on a 120-acre Eastside parcel that included Syrah, Mourvèdre, and Cabernet Sauvignon vineyards. "We did some amateur blending with these three varietals and made our first wine in 1999," recalls Brady. Although the property was rundown, most of the vineyards were in good condition. Those stricken with the phylloxera louse were pulled out and replaced with new vineyards. Brady and Blackwell later purchased a twenty-five-acre parcel that came with vineyards and a house, which is now the tasting room.

The majority of the acreage is planted to Rhône varietals and the balance to Cabernet Sauvignon, Cabernet Franc, Petit Verdot, and Malbec. An acre near the Blackwell-Brady residence, also on the property, is planted to Tinta Cão, Tinta Roriz, and Touriga Nacional, Portuguese varietals that go into Clautiere's fragrant port. As Clautiere's winemaker, Brady learned technical skills at the University of California at Davis and picked up the nuances of winemaking by working with two known local winemakers, veteran John Munch and young renegade Matt Trevisan.

At Clautiere, you'll sample the Estate Mon Beau Rouge, a dark, rich blend of Syrah, Counoise, Grenache, and Mourvèdre, with a touch of Viognier. The Estate Grand Rouge exudes bright cherry notes and is the same blend as Mon Beau Rouge, with the addition of Cabernet Sauvignon. Clautiere also produces single-varietal Cabernet Sauvignon, Syrah, and Viognier. All wines are made from estate fruit grown on the fifty-seven-acre vineyard property.

A festive atmosphere permeates the tasting room, with an assortment of gifts and wigs for sale. The room is also stocked with cheeses, baguettes, and cured meats that can be enjoyed as a light picnic in the garden. If you're looking for more than just a tasting visit, check out the R-rated performances at Clautiere's winemaker dinners. Usually a drag show or a cabaret, the events are staged adjacent to the tasting room in a theater that was once a barn, built in the 1930s. The winery also hosts monthly movie nights where Rhône wines are served with popcorn. Before you leave the grounds, stop at the small red and black cabin in the garden to see your distorted image in the three funhouse mirrors. You will fondly remember this visit as tasting Rhônes with a touch of "ruckus."

CLAUTIERE VINEYARD // 1340 Penman Springs Road, Paso Robles, CA 93446

T 805.237.3789
F 805.237.1730
E info@clautiere.com

www.clautiere.com

ACCESS
From Highway 101, exit at Highway 46 East. Go east for 2.5 miles and turn right on Union Road, then make first immediate left, following Union Road. Drive 2.5 miles to Penman Springs Road. Turn right and go just over .5 mile. Winery is on right.

Hours for visits and tastings:
Noon – 5PM daily.
Closed on major holidays.

Wheelchair access.

TASTINGS & TOURS
Charge for tastings: $5 for eight wines; includes logo glass.

Tours by appointment only.

Typical wines offered: Rhône varietals and blends, Cabernet Sauvignon, and port.

Wine-related items for sale.

PICNICS & PROGRAMS
Picnic area open to public. Picnic ingredients sold in tasting room.

Special events: Annual cabaret show. Check website for event calendar.

Wine club.

Eberle Winery

OWNER: GARY EBERLE // WINEMAKER: BEN MAYO

If you detect the aroma of barbecue wafting down Highway 46 East, you'll know Gary Eberle is behind the grill conveniently stationed in front of the tasting room. "I love to barbecue," Eberle says, "and when the mood moves me, I'll pull out twenty-five tri-tips, a case of ribs, and eighteen pounds of duck sausage from the freezer." When not on the road promoting his wines, Eberle indulges in his culinary passion two or three times a month, much to the surprise of the visitors, who are delighted to savor the grilled meats with Eberle's signature Syrah and Cabernet Sauvignon.

The founder of Eberle Winery has made his mark in the Paso region as a pioneer of Syrah plantings and cofounder of the Paso Robles appellation established in 1980. Eberle was introduced to Shiraz wine (the Australian Syrah) by an Aussie winemaker while at the University of California at Davis in the 1970s. At the time, this grape was not widely available in the United States. UC Davis was one of the few places where Eberle could obtain the Syrah budwood, which originally came from Chapoutier Winery's plantings in the Northern Rhône. He planted twenty acres of the French Syrah in 1975 at Estrella River Winery (now Meridian Vineyards and Winery). He named it the Estrella clone after the winery he cofounded in 1973. By 1978, Eberle was making history as the first winemaker in the United States to produce 100 percent Syrah. It's believed that a good percentage of this grape grown in California can be traced to Eberle's original plantings.

How did the former biology student and defensive tackle for the Pennsylvania State University football team find himself in the wine business? In those days he enjoyed sipping Mateus, a cheap Portuguese wine then popular in the United States. A professor who was an enophile introduced Eberle to the pleasures of Bordeaux. "We were listening to an opera and I had an epiphany," he recalls. At the time, Eberle was partway through his dissertation and aiming for a career in medical research. Instead, he headed for UC Davis. "I was young and foolish but I never looked back," recalls Eberle, whose chemistry background made for an easy transition to enology.

Although Eberle wanted to be a winemaker, he never thought he would own a winery. He came to Paso in the early 1970s on the suggestion of his professor at UC Davis, who told him that it was the next great red wine region. After working for nine years at Estrella River Winery, which produced 500,000 cases annually, Eberle yearned to start a winery under his name, one with a much smaller production. Noted vintner Howard Steinbeck of Steinbeck Vineyards suggested that Eberle establish his winery on the Steinbeck ranch. He took the offer, but only to plant his Estrella Syrah, which he did in partnership with Steinbeck.

To start a winery and tasting room, Eberle favored the busy Highway 46 East thoroughfare. In 1983, he purchased a forty-acre estate a short distance south of Steinbeck Vineyards. A year later, he opened Eberle Winery, a ranch-style winery on Paso's 46 East corridor. On this estate, Eberle planted Cabernet Sauvignon, Muscat Canelli, and Chardonnay vineyards. The Syrah, Zinfandel, and Barbera are planted on the Steinbeck Vineyards, and the Viognier on the adjacent Mill Road Vineyards. About 80 percent of the fruit from these three vineyards is sold to other producers. Steinbeck remains Eberle's partner in the winery as well as the Steinbeck and Mill Road vineyards.

Eberle's philosophy of "do as little damage to the grapes as possible" is followed by winemaker Ben Mayo. The Estate Cabernet Sauvignon, aged for eighteen months in American oak, is rich with cassis and black cherry. The very best of all the Cabernet Sauvignon barrels, declared only in exceptional vintages, is bottled as Reserve Estate Cabernet Sauvignon. Since the start of the winery, only twelve vintages of this wine have been released. The wine is aged for twenty-four months in barrels and then five years in bottles before its release. The Steinbeck Syrah is loaded with black fruit, and the robust Zinfandel from Remo Belli's thirty-five-year-old vineyard explodes with berry flavors and peppery spice.

Decorated with a plethora of awards and medals, the Eberle tasting room is a bustling place. Since *Eberle*

EBERLE WINERY // 2459/3810 Highway 46 East, Paso Robles, CA 93447

T 805.238.9607
F 805.237.0344
E tastingroom@eberlewinery.com

www.eberlewinery.com

ACCESS
From Highway 101, take Highway 46 East exit and go east for 3 miles. Winery is on left.

Hours for visits and tastings:
Open daily 10AM–5PM winter,
10AM–6PM summer.
Closed on major holidays.

Wheelchair access.

TASTINGS & TOURS
Charge for tasting: first five wines complimentary. After that, $2.50 includes glass and 20 percent discount on wine purchase.

Free general tour scheduled every thirty minutes, starting at 10:30AM, with last tour at 5:30 or 4:30PM depending on time of year. Two-hour $20 VIP tour, by appointment, includes private wine and cheese tasting in the cellar. Contact Gary DeRose at 805.238.9606, ext. 210.

Typical wines offered: Syrah, Cabernet Sauvignon, Zinfandel, Roussanne, Viognier, Barbera, Sangiovese, Chardonnay, Syrah rosé, and Muscat Canelli.

Wine-related items for sale.

PICNICS & PROGRAMS
Picnic area open to public. No picnic ingredients sold in tasting room. Picnic baskets can be delivered by local restaurants.

Special events: Monthly guest chef dinners. Check website for event calendar.

Wine club.

in German means "small boar," the entrance has a replica of a bronze Porcellino boar. The original, cast in 1620, is in the Straw Market in Florence, Italy. You'll notice people rubbing the boar's nose (considered good luck) and tossing coins in the fountain below (donated to a local children's charity). Cabernet and Roussanne, Eberle's black standard poodles, might come over to greet you. On occasion, you'll see Gary Eberle, dressed casually in shorts and T-shirt, pouring himself a glass of Cabernet Sauvignon at the tasting counter.

Eberle's popular guided tour, both informative and fun, takes you through the production facility and down to the sixteen-hundred-square-foot caves, home to twelve hundred to seventeen hundred barrels of French and American oak. From the arched ceiling of the damp, dark caves hang soda straws, icicle-like formations made of mineral deposits. The caves also serve as a dramatic setting for Eberle's special events and candle-lit dinners in the Wild Boar Room, a big draw among wine aficionados. If you are unable to attend an Eberle special event, you can enjoy your own feast on the redwood deck overlooking the vineyards. With a forty-eight-hour advance notice, Eberle's tasting room will arrange lunch from one of Paso's restaurants, including Bistro Laurent, whose gourmet picnic baskets are filled with delicacies to savor on the redwood deck with Eberle's luscious reds.

Founded by Italian brothers Phil and Frank Arciero, EOS Estate Winery is named for a Greek goddess. According to legend, Eos opened the gates of heaven every morning to the chariot of the sun, heralding the dawn. Since Orion was one of Eos's lovers, that constellation appears with the image of the goddess on the wine label. A fifty-foot mural of the design hangs in the tasting room. For the Arciero family, the symbol of the goddess serves as more than an artistic statement. It signifies the winery's dawn harvest, when grapes are picked at the peak of freshness and flavor. The mythological theme continues in vineyard blocks named after relatives of the goddess: Astraeus, Zephyrus, and Notus.

The Arcieros, owners of a Los Angeles construction company that built parts of the Los Angeles airport and Marina Del Rey, purchased the two-hundred-acre property (since expanded to seven hundred acres) in 1982. They were introduced to Paso Robles on a visit to look for home development sites. Paso reminded the Arcieros of their Italian hometown near the monastery of Montecassino. This inspired them to construct a winery replicating the monastery, complete with a campanile. A winery, under the name of Arciero Vineyards, was established in 1985. In the mid-1990s, the Arcieros took on partners Vernon Underwood and Kerry Vix, the winery's general manager. Under the new management, the EOS label was launched. The changes also brought an expansion on the property, including the 24,000-square-foot barrel storage room.

The sprawling vineyards make a spectacular sight, running almost two miles along Highway 46 East. Ten grape varieties are planted in three large blocks, predominantly to Chardonnay, Cabernet Sauvignon, and Merlot, with the balance dedicated to Zinfandel, Petite Sirah, Muscat Canelli, Cabernet Franc, Pinot Grigio, Petit Verdot, and Malbec. Paying homage to their heritage, the Arcieros have planted Italian varietals as well: ten acres of Nebbiolo and sixteen of Sangiovese. These are bottled as single varietals and as Arpeggio, a blend of the two with a little Zinfandel. EOS follows a unique vineyard practice crucial to the health of young vines. Prior to planting, each vineyard row is trenched five feet deep with a backhoe to mix the deeper, old soil with the softer, more porous topsoil. This promotes vertical penetration of the roots into the soil.

In the midst of the vast vineyard landscape sits the 104,000-square-foot Romanesque winery anchored by a majestic fountain, a popular backdrop for wedding celebrations. Once inside, you can embark on a self-guided tour, where informative wall panels explain the winemaking process. The tour continues upstairs along a hallway where you get a good look at the enologist's laboratory and the bottling room. The tour ends on the balcony with a sweeping view of the vineyards and the town of Paso in the distance. At harvest time, you can experience the excitement of the crush pad from this vantage point as grapes are unloaded to

start the crushing process. If you're so inclined, you are encouraged to go below to taste the grapes.

The winery's annual production of more than 100,000 cases is bottled under three labels. The flagship is EOS, with wines that don't make the cut going into 10,000 cases of Novella. A third tier, the Arciero series, is a small production of mostly rosé, available in the tasting room only.

Winemaker Leslie Melendez concentrates on food-friendly wines ready to drink on release. However, the Reserve and Cupa Grandis wines are worthy of cellaring for a few years. The Cupa Grandis series under the EOS label is part of the Grand Barrel Reserve program, wines that feature grapes from the very best of EOS estate vineyards. The Cupa Grandis Chardonnay is aged 100 percent in Louis Latour French oak, from Burgundy's famed barrel producer. Cupa Grandis Petite Sirah is aged for up to eighteen months in barrels made from specific forests in France and the United States.

In the reserve category, you'll taste the spicy Petite Sirah, blended with different Bordeaux varietals, depending on the vintage. The Reserve Fumé Blanc is redolent with melon and pineapple aromas, while the Chardonnay has hints of tropical fruits balanced with crisp acidity. The regular tasting lineup ranges from Sauvignon Blanc, Chardonnay, and Pinot Grigio to Merlot, Cabernet Sauvignon, Cabernet Franc, and Zinfandel. If you enjoy dessert wine, the heady honeysuckle aroma of EOS Estate Late Harvest Moscato is a perfect finish to any meal.

A parade of tall cypress trees stands guard along the winery's driveway. Inside the expansive tasting room, you'll see a large lounge on your right. Part of the décor includes a red racing car, a memento from the Arciero Racing Company. Frank Arciero fielded his first racing team in 1957. The tradition has continued through the second and third generations, who compete in championship races.

The EOS tasting room is appropriately named the Mediterranean Marketplace, well-stocked with Italian ceramics, gourmet items, cookbooks, and apparel. The deli case holds cold cuts, cheeses, and fresh sandwiches made daily. You can picnic indoors or outdoors, including the fountain area. On a warm afternoon, visitors perch on the fountain's edge and dangle their feet in the cool sprinkles. ⌁

EOS ESTATE WINERY // 5625 Highway 46 East, Paso Robles, CA 93446

T 805.239.2562
F 805.239.2317
E info@eosvintage.com

www.eosvintage.com

ACCESS
From Highway 101, exit at Highway 46 East and drive east for 4 miles. Winery is on right.

Hours for visits and tastings:
10AM–5PM daily; to 6PM on summer weekends. Closed major holidays.

Wheelchair access.

TASTINGS & TOURS
Charge for tasting: Most wines complimentary; $7 for reserve and library wines includes logo glass.

Daily self-guided tour of production facility. VIP tour by appointment only. $7 includes barrel and counter tasting; $20 tour includes a box lunch and barrel and counter tasting.

Typical wines offered: Sauvignon Blanc, Chardonnay, Merlot, Zinfandel, Cabernet Sauvignon, Pinot Grigio, and late harvest wines.

Wine-related items for sale.

PICNICS & PROGRAMS
Picnic area open to public. Picnic ingredients sold in tasting room.

Special events: Check website for event calendar.

Wine club.

Justin Vineyards & Winery

OWNERS: JUSTIN & DEBORAH BALDWIN // WINEMAKER: FRED HOLLOWAY

When you visit Justin Vineyards & Winery, you will taste the delicious, deep rich Bordeaux blends, tour the winery's Isosceles Center, have a wine country lunch at Deborah's Room, and perhaps even stay the weekend at the winery's luxuriously romantic French-style inn. But first, you must carefully step over Zamboni, the winery's Labrador retriever, who on most days is stretched out like a welcome mat at the tasting room entrance.

Proprietors Justin and Deborah Baldwin left the financial industry for the wine business. She was a mortgage banker; he was an investment banker. Both adored Bordeaux wines. "We love wine. It was a pas-sion that grew into a hobby that grew into a business," says Deborah. Their goal, she admits, was to make a red blend modeled after Bordeaux's famed Châteaux Margaux. The couple purchased the 160-acre property in 1981 in Paso's remote Adelaida Valley. A year later they planted seventy-two acres to the three classic Bordeaux varietals—Cabernet Sauvignon, Cabernet Franc, and Merlot—along with some Chardonnay. Since then, plantings of Syrah, Sangiovese, Nebbiolo, and Orange Muscat have been added. Justin's first vintage of 1987 was released in 1990 with a production of 1,500 cases. They thought they'd wind up making 10,000 cases a year, but the production kept doubling each year. It has now grown to 60,000 cases annually.

Winemaker Fred Holloway's philosophy is straightforward. The wine should express the *terroir*: the sum entity of soil composition, microclimate, exposure, and altitude that has a profound effect on the taste and quality of the wine. Because of Paso's diverse climate, the Westside wine region is five to eight degrees Fahrenheit cooler (beneficial for Pinot Noir but not for Cabernet Sauvignon) than Paso's Eastside region. Surprisingly, Bordeaux varietals do well on Justin's property, which is on the west side of Paso. "We get a little more sun because of the high elevation," notes the winemaker. The region's fog breaks a little earlier, allowing for more warmth during the day. Justin's vineyards are at elevations ranging from sixteen hundred to twenty-three hundred feet, which further adds to daytime warmth, says Holloway. Since the vineyards are located on the east side of the Santa Lucia Mountains, they are also protected from the cool coastal winds. The soil on Justin's property is rich with fertile clay—not ideal for grapes. But it also contains limestone, which inhibits aggressive growth and creates a more concentrated fruit. The presence of limestone, therefore, balances the effects of fertile clay and creates what Holloway calls a "yin-yang" effect.

You can taste the intensity of the hillside fruit in Isosceles, Justin's flagship wine—a deep, rich blend of Cabernet Sauvignon, Merlot, and Cabernet Franc. The wine is aged in the barrels for nineteen months and further aged in bottles for nine months before release—bottle-aging integrates the wine's flavors and helps it mature. The ruby red Justification, on the other hand, is a blend of Cabernet Franc and Merlot. Other Justin wines include Sauvignon Blanc, Chardonnay, Cabernet, Syrah, and a port-style wine, called Obtuse, made from Cabernet Sauvignon.

Besides its Bordeaux varietals, Justin is noted for its forty-minute Sensory Evaluation/Barrel Tasting tour, which takes you through the caves of the Isosceles Center. You are treated to a barrel tasting so you can compare wine aged in oak from different regions and barrel makers, and new oak compared with wine aged in old oak. You then move to the top of the Center, on to the Sensory Evaluation Room. Here, you use professional evaluation tools and techniques at the blending table and learn how to properly taste, smell, and identify the aromas in the wine. The center's luxurious lounge serves as a venue for the winery's special events. An intimate alcove in the barrel room, adorned by a wrought-iron gate, is dedicated to reserve tastings.

Justin's farmhouses, topped with bright yellow awnings and accented with geranium-filled window boxes, are clustered among the oak-studded hills and the vineyards. The exquisitely landscaped grounds feature a lush rose garden surrounding a water fountain shaded by a grape arbor. Step inside the reception area of the tasting room, and you're embraced by the warm Provençal colors of ocher and burnt red. You then pass through a handsome wrought-iron gate and head for the tasting room appointed with handsome Oriental rugs covering limestone floors. Handcrafted wooden bins cradling wine bottles line the walls.

JUSTIN VINEYARDS & WINERY // 1680 Chimney Rock Road, Paso Robles, CA 93446

T 805.238.6932
F 805.237.4152
E info@JUSTINwine.com

www.JUSTINwine.com

ACCESS
From Highway 101, take Highway 46 East exit. Head west on 24th Street and drive 19 miles to the winery. (24th Street turns into G14, also named Nacimiento Lake Road, leading to Chimney Rock Road.)

Hours for visits and tasting:
10AM–5PM daily.
Closed on major holidays.

Wheelchair access.

TASTINGS & TOURS
Charge for tasting: $5 for five wines; includes logo glass.

Tours daily at 10:30AM and 2:30PM for $10; includes wine tasting.

Typical wines offered: Bordeaux-style blends, Cabernet Sauvignon, Syrah, Chardonnay, Sauvignon Blanc, and dessert wines.

Wine-related items for sale.

PICNICS & PROGRAMS
Picnic area open to public. Picnic ingredients sold in tasting room. Deborah's Room restaurant open for lunch on Saturday and Sunday. Call ahead for picnic baskets.

Special events: Guest chef dinners. Check website for event calendar.

Wine club.

The tasting begins with a crisp and minerally Sauvignon Blanc and Chardonnay, and takes you through the rich and luscious Syrahs and Cabernet Sauvignons, ending with the decadent Obtuse. To heighten the pleasures of this wine's bittersweet chocolate flavors, the Obtuse is paired with a sampling of rich dark chocolate.

Justin is the only winery in the Paso area to offer fine dining, in its Deborah's Room restaurant. You can treat yourself to wine-country cuisine served outdoors by the wishing-well patio. The lunch prepared by chef Ryan Swarthout will consist mostly of freshly picked herbs and vegetables from Justin's garden just behind the kitchen. ⚘

L'Aventure Winery

OWNER / WINEMAKER: STEPHAN ASSEO

Stephan Asseo is among the band of free-spirited, renegade winemakers who have pioneered the trend of Super Paso – a blend of Bordeaux and Rhône varietals. In 1997, the Bordeaux native left his hometown of Saint-Emilion, the famed Bordeaux wine village, seeking new territory to make his style of wine – a blend of Bordeaux and Rhône varietals – a practice strictly forbidden in both regions. His quest took him from Spain and Italy to South Africa, Lebanon, and finally California. In his wanderings, Asseo searched for a region that would embrace his maverick ideas. He found it in Paso. Coming from France's traditional background, Asseo discovered what he calls an "intellectual freshness" in Paso's mix of winemakers, both old-timers and newcomers, and an open attitude toward experimentation. "Paso winemakers are not prisoners of the past. We are free to do what we think is best for our *terroir*." For a Frenchman *terroir* is a sacred word. It's more than an expression of the earth, it's the confluence of climate, altitude, and exposure that defines the individual character of the grape and therefore the wine.

When Asseo first saw Paso, he was entranced by the foothills of the Santa Lucia Mountains. "I was looking for a wilderness area and found this magical, wild, and virginal spot in the middle of nowhere." The 127-acre property on Paso's west side was at the end of a dirt road. It had no driveway or vineyards. Asseo chose it for its proximity to the ocean and for its microclimate – early-morning fog followed by warm days and cool nights, thanks to the maritime influence of the Templeton Gap. Asseo purchased the property and established L'Aventure in 1997. His first vintage of 1998 was produced from purchased grapes; by 2000, wines were produced from estate fruit supplemented with some purchased grapes.

The property surrounding the winery is spread out on the hillsides, with the highest vineyard planted at an elevation of twenty-four hundred feet. The majority of vineyards are planted with Syrah (35 percent), followed by Cabernet Sauvignon (25 percent) and small quantities of Viognier, Roussanne, Grenache, and Mourvèdre. Asseo also planted a whopping 18 percent of Petit Verdot (the red grape used minimally in Bordeaux blends), which he calls his wild card. "It's rare to plant such a large percentage of Petit Verdot, but I believe in it," he says.

For Asseo, this grape adds a classic style to the fleshy nuances of Cabernet Sauvignon or Syrah. Petit Verdot matures late but is not as exuberant as Cabernet Sauvignon or Syrah. It's an ideal grape for the soil, which includes rocky limestone and is calcareous (alkaline in nature due to the presence of calcium carbonate, which gives the wine a ripe character) with traces of clay. The combination acts like a sponge, storing water during the rainy season and releasing it to the roots during the dry season, allowing the soil to stay moist longer and leading to a late harvest. The longer the cycle of maturation between veraison – when grapes soften, accumulate sugar, and lessen acidity – and harvest, the more complex the fruit.

L'Aventure's thirty-acre vineyard produces around eight thousand cases annually. Asseo's winemaking philosophy is simple: good wine is made not in the barrels, but in the vineyards. According to Asseo, if you start with good fruit, it's easy to make good wine. But, he emphasizes, you cannot make good wine from mediocre fruit. He believes in high-density planting of twenty-one hundred vines per acre and a low yield of about two tons of fruit per acre, as opposed to a normal yield of four to five tons per acre. More vines per acre results in a smaller yield, because the vines have to struggle for nutrition and growth. "A small production means the vine will take better care of the fruit and give concentrated fruit," Asseo explains. "Whatever the varietal, the grape will have intense flavor and better ripeness."

L'Aventure wines are bold with tannins – a tactile sensation that can be described as astringent, but that mellows with age. Tannins are derived from the red grape's skins, pits, and stems and give the red wine its age potential. Far from astringent, Asseo's wines have soft, lush tannins, giving the wine a long, rich finish. To achieve this, Asseo enforces a tough viticultural regime. His team paces the vineyards more than fifteen

L'AVENTURE WINERY / STEPHAN VINEYARDS // 2815 Live Oak Road, Paso Robles, CA 93446

T 805.227.1588
F 805.227.6988
E stephanwines@tcsn.net

www.aventurewine.com

ACCESS
From Highway 101, take Highway 46 West exit and go west for 1 mile. Turn right on Arbor Road, which becomes Live Oak Road, then turns to gravel. Continue to end and cross two cattle guards. Of three gates, green one leads to winery. If gate is closed, punch code written on box.

Hours for visits and tastings:
11AM – 4PM Thursday – Sunday.
By appointment Monday – Wednesday.
Closed on major holidays.

Wheelchair access.

TASTINGS & TOURS
Charge for tasting: $10 for five or six wines; includes glass.

Tours for groups of five or more. No tours after 3PM.

Typical wines offered: Roussanne, blends of Cabernet and Syrah, Rhône blends, single-varietal Syrah and Cabernet Sauvignon.

Wine-related items for sale.

PICNICS & PROGRAMS
No picnic area open to public.

Special events: Check website for event calendar.

Wine club.

times during the season, pulling leaves, training canopies, hedging, and performing other maintenance, to arrive at perfectly mature fruit. Asseo also controls the yield by picking only the best fruit and dropping some on the ground. A mere two to three pounds of fruit might be picked from each vine, compared with a normal yield of eight to ten pounds per vine. Depending on the varietal, this low yield might result in only one bottle per vine.

As a master blender, Asseo usually starts with fifteen different combinations of Bordeaux and Rhône varietals, complementing the mix with a touch of Zinfandel. After a series of tastings, he narrows the selection to about six blends. At that point, he invites local winemakers and wine aficionados for a blind tasting to help choose the blend of the vintage. Over the years, the most popular blend has been the fifty-fifty Syrah and Cabernet Sauvignon blend with a splash of Zinfandel, bottled as Optimus. In the L'Aventure Estate Cuvée blend, the Zinfandel is replaced by Petit Verdot. L'Aventure Cuvée Côte Estate is an archetypal Rhône blend of Mourvèdre, Syrah, and Grenache. But the winery is not dedicated to blends only: it bottles single varietals of Cabernet Sauvignon and Syrah.

Getting to L'Aventure is an adventure in itself. The winery entrance begins at the security gate, where long, rugged Live Oak Road leads into the gravel road and past the cattle guards. L'Aventure's winery and tasting room is housed in a large warehouse. You won't find a typical tasting room. There are no T-shirts and gourmet foods for sale—only the wines, glassware, and decanters. People who make the trek to L'Aventure come simply to taste the wines. ◠◡

Martin & Weyrich winery has carved out a niche for its portfolio of Cal-Italia wines, so if you are an aficionado of Italian wines, you're in for a treat. The sun-drenched Tuscan-style tasting room at the corner of Buena Vista Road and Highway 46 East is among Paso's landmarks. From a distance, you can spot the colorful patio umbrellas that dot the terrace of the vine-draped tasting room.

Brothers Tom and Nick Martin, joined by their brother-in-law David Weyrich, established the Martin Brothers Winery in 1981 with a hundred-acre property on the east side of Paso. During his college days, Tom Martin, a southern California native, got his first taste of Nebbiolo on a trip to Florence. Bottled as Barolo wine in Italy, Nebbiolo is the primary grape of the Piedmont region. So passionate was he about this grape that when the brothers acquired the vineyards, they planted 8.3 acres of this varietal in 1982 on their Estate ranch. Although Nebbiolo had been grown in the Central Valley since the 1970s, it was bottled as jug wine. However, the Martin brothers produced it as a fine wine, and since then the Martin & Weyrich Winery has gained a reputation as one of the foremost producers of Nebbiolo in the United States. As interest in this varietal spread, other California vintners got on the Nebbiolo bandwagon, and by the late 1980s varietals such as Sangiovese and Pinot Grigio were also planted. This burst of Italian varietals earned itself the moniker of Cal-Italia – Italian varietals planted in California.

Martin & Weyrich produces only three thousand cases a year of the Nebbiolo wine, as it can be a difficult varietal to cultivate, says winemaker Craig Reed. "If you don't grow it properly it can overcrop, and the grapes can lack color and have aggressive tannins that can add an astringent taste to the wine," notes Reed. Too much sunlight on the fruit bleaches it and too little adds vegetal flavors – an unpleasant bell-peppery taste. But for Martin & Weyrich, this grape is truly a labor of love.

The Martin Brothers Winery became Martin & Weyrich in 1998, when David and Mary Weyrich purchased it from the Martin family. Currently, three hundred acres are planted to Italian varietals, such as Nebbiolo, Sangiovese, Muscat Canelli, and Pinot Grigio, along with Cabernet Sauvignon, Pinot Noir, Petit Verdot, Chardonnay, and Rhône varietals. The plantings are spread out in three ranches: the Winery Estate, the Weyrich Ranch in southeast Paso, and Jack Ranch in Edna Valley.

Although not Italian, Reed and co-winemaker Alan Kinne understand the nuances of Italian wines and share a philosophy. "We like to make elegant wines that are not heavy, over-extracted, and over-the-top," says Reed. Over-extracted wine, Reed explains, is the result of grapes that are picked overripe and thus give a jammy, raisiny character and deliver a wine high in alcohol. But aren't Italian red wines known to be big and bold? "I think Italian wines are a different kind of big than Californian," counters Kinne. He cites the example of Super Tuscan, a blend of Sangiovese and Merlot that is a big, bold wine but still very elegant. The winemakers point out that Italian wines are made to be food-friendly.

Martin & Weyrich's highly popular tasting room is stocked with Italian gourmet products, along with exquisite Deruta pottery and Palio flags (the banners of Siena's famed horse race). Colorfully wrapped bottles protrude from the wall racks, each rolled in paper corresponding to the bottle's color-coded top. At the tasting counter, you'll sample Insieme (Italian for "together"), Martin & Weyrich's New World blend of old-world grapes grown in California. Rich with spice, pepper, and berry flavors, Insieme is a blend of Sangiovese, Nebbiolo, Zinfandel, Cabernet Sauvignon, and Barbera. The Etrusco Cabernet is blended with Sangiovese, the popular grape of Tuscany. The Nebbiolo is redolent with aromas of cherry, rose, spice, and truffles, and the reserve Nebbiolo Vecchio (Italian for "old") is aged in select barrels and produced in a limited quantity. Dolcetto (also from Piedmont) exudes flavors of fresh strawberries and makes a good sipping wine for summer afternoons. The signature Sangiovese Il Palio is named after the noted Sienese horse race. Besides the Italian varietals, you can sample Bordeaux and Rhône varietals as well

MARTIN & WEYRICH WINERY // 2610 Buena Vista Drive, Paso Robles, CA 93446

T 805.238.2520
F 805.238.0887
E sales@martinweyrich.com

www.martinweyrich.com

ACCESS
From Highway 101, take Highway 46 East exit. Go .5 mile east to Buena Vista Drive. Winery is on corner of 46 East and Buena Vista.

Hours for visits and tastings:
10AM – 5PM Sunday – Thursday.
10AM – 6PM Friday – Saturday.
Closed on major holidays.

Wheelchair access.

TASTINGS & TOURS
Charge for tasting: Different levels range from $2 to $5, reimbursed with wine purchase.

Tours by appointment only.

Typical wines offered: Chardonnays from Edna Valley, Hidden Valley, and Huerhuero Creek, Pinot Grigio, Nebbiolo, Insieme, Sangiovese, Zinfandel, Cabernet Etrusco, and Moscato Allegro.

Wine-related items for sale.

PICNICS & PROGRAMS
Picnic area open to public. Picnic ingredients sold in tasting room.

Special events: Christmas and other holiday events held in December, cooking classes at Villa Toscana, and barbecues and other seasonal events. Check website for event calendar.

Wine club.

as Zinfandel, bottled under two labels: La Primitiva, a blend of four vineyards in the Santa Lucia Mountains, and the Dante Dusi vineyard-designated label, which has fruit from one of Paso's sought-after vineyards, planted in 1946.

In 2001, the Weyrich family purchased York Mountain Winery, Paso's oldest winery. Built in 1882 of unreinforced masonry, the winery was condemned for earthquake retrofitting. Plans are to rebuild the winery and tasting room with a museum above. The winemaker's residence will be converted into a bed-and-breakfast. York Mountain wine will continue to be produced at Martin & Weyrich Winery, and the wines will be available in its tasting room. The thirty-acre vineyard that lay in disrepair will be replanted to Pinot Noir and Portuguese varietals.

About half a mile from the bustle of the tasting room sits Martin & Weyrich's Villa Toscana, a lavish Tuscan-style building with gardens and fountains. Named after Italian grape varietals, all eight of the luxurious suites in the bed-and-breakfast have panoramic views of vineyards planted to Nebbiolo, Cabernet Sauvignon, and Sangiovese. For those seeking privacy, there's a two-bedroom gated cottage with a private patio. The inn's chef, Richard Graham, prepares a hearty country breakfast for guests, and in the afternoon sets out a lavish spread of appetizers paired with Martin & Weyrich wines. If you're unable to get a reservation, you can still savor the Tuscan experience at one of Martin & Weyrich Winery's special events held at the villa.

Robert Hall Winery

OWNERS: ROBERT L. HALL & MARGARET BURRELL // WINEMAKER: DON BRADY

More than a state-of-the-art winery, Robert Hall is a hospitality center, an entertainment venue, a culinary institute, and, above all, an architectural delight, designed by Tim Mark Woodle of Steven D. Pults, AIA, & Associates. The multiarched brick building sits majestically amid lush gardens and fountains surrounded by Syrah and Cabernet Sauvignon vineyards. Owner Robert Hall recalls the inspiration for his building: "When I was in Europe thirty-five years ago, I saw a monastery that had arches like this, and I knew that one day when I had a winery, I wanted it designed this way."

With business ventures ranging from retail and restaurants to bowling centers and travel agencies, Hall traveled extensively. However, it was on a family trip to France in the late 1970s that Hall first visited the Rhône Valley. So captivated was he by the Rhône varietal that he wished to establish his own winery. He embarked on his quest in the 1980s, and after several years of researching different appellations in California, he settled on Paso in the mid-1990s, for the region's soil, water, and weather. "We have more days favorable to our business, plus we have twenty-five million feet of water underground," asserts Hall. Although located on the east side of Paso, known for its warm climate, the vineyards are planted on the southern banks of the Estrella River and therefore experience a more moderate temperature. The vineyards also benefit from the cool nights influenced by the coastal winds that Paso is so well known for.

In 1995, Hall purchased a 165-acre property and named it Home Vineyard. The first vintage of 1999 was produced in a winemaking facility in Paso and released in 2001. That same year, the winery was built and Don Brady came on board as the winemaker. The elaborate tasting room and Hospitality Center on the winery grounds opened in 2005. Providing the bulk of the winery's production, Home Vineyard is located due east of the winery and planted to Cabernet Sauvignon, Zinfandel, Sauvignon Blanc, Chardonnay, Merlot, and Syrah. Two other vineyards have been added to Home Vineyard, and the three-vineyard property is collectively known as Hall Ranch and now totals 300 acres planted to twelve varietals. Situated on a rolling terrace above the southern bank of the Estrella River, the 110-acre Terrace Vineyard is planted to both Bordeaux and Rhône varietals. The 25-acre Bench Vineyard, planted to Cabernet Sauvignon and Syrah, wraps around the winery on a coastal bench that overlooks the Huerhuero Creek. The Bench Vineyard's decomposed granite soil allows for good drainage, which results in the vines' low yield and produces Robert Hall's most intense and concentrated fruit.

Robert Hall wines are ready to drink when young but also show age potential. The portfolio includes Bordeaux and Rhône varietals, with a strong focus on the Rhône program. The signature wine is Rhône de Robles, a blend of Grenache and Syrah with small amounts of Cinsault and Counoise. The Rosé de Robles is a refreshing blend of Syrah and Grenache, with a touch of Mourvèdre. As is common with Paso winemakers, Don Brady likes to marry Rhône and Bordeaux varietals. Laced with aromas of black currant and cedar, the 2004 Cabernet Sauvignon has small amounts of Cabernet Franc and Merlot and 6 percent of Syrah. "The Syrah is soft and voluptuous and adds a middle body to the wine," Brady says. The Merlot has some Cabernet Sauvignon and Cabernet Franc, with a dash of Zinfandel that exudes hints of brambleberry—a commonly used term that describes the nuances of blackberry, boysenberry, raspberry, and olallieberry.

Among the white wines, the Sauvignon Blanc is refreshing, like biting into a crisp apple, while the Chardonnay is smooth, with rich butterscotch notes. For port aficionados, there's a limited production (six hundred cases annually) of vintage port made from the four traditional Portuguese varietals: Touriga, Souzão, Tinta Cão, and Alvarelhão. The wine is fortified with brandy and aged for twenty-four months in large Portuguese pipes, or oak barrels.

The highlight of the spacious tasting room is the elaborate nine-foot-tall chandelier designed by vineyard manager Richard Raper, crafted from steel tubing and accented with grape-leaf motifs made of cast iron. In a collaborative effort, everyone at the winery worked on the piece, from staff members to Hall's wife, Margaret Burrell, and artist Steve Kalar. From the cherry and mahogany bar, you'll enjoy an expansive view of Paso through thirteen-foot-high windows. Upstairs, you'll get another spectacular view of Paso from the viewing tower.

The twenty-minute tour will take you through the winery grounds and down to the impressive caves, home to some four thousand barrels. You'll notice some very large barrels with a 120-gallon capacity. Made of Portuguese wood, they are used for the port wines. The barrel room, seating 225, is a perfect venue for special events and winemaker dinners. The dramatic hanging lamps of canvas and metal are the result of an artistic collaboration between Burrell and Kalar.

You might end up spending the better part of your day here, not just tasting wines but playing a game of bocce, taking a culinary or wine appreciation class, and perhaps ending your day in the amphitheater, rocking to the beat of a concert or dancing under the stars. ⚲

ROBERT HALL WINERY // 3443 Mill Road, Paso Robles, CA 93446

T 805.239.1616
F 805.239.2464
E info@roberthallwinery.com

www.roberthallwinery.com

ACCESS
From Highway 101, take Highway 46 East exit and go east for 2 miles. Winery is on right.

Hours for visits and tastings:
Open daily 10AM–6PM summer,
10AM–5PM winter.
Closed on major holidays.

Wheelchair access.

TASTINGS & TOURS
Charge for tasting: $5; reserve wine tasting $8.

Daily tours on the hour.

Typical wines offered: Sauvignon Blanc, Chardonnay, Rosé de Robles, Rhône blends, Grenache, Syrah, Cabernet Sauvignon, Merlot, Bordeaux-style blends, port, and Orange Muscat.

Wine-related items for sale.

PICNICS & PROGRAMS
Picnic area open to public. Picnic ingredients sold in tasting room.

Special events: Winemaker dinners and wine and cooking seminars with guest chefs. Check website for event calendar.

Wine club.

Bursts of wildflowers strike a contrast against the white picket fence that circles the picturesque property of Summerwood Winery and its adjacent inn. Formerly the tasting room of Treana Winery, the farmhouse building was acquired in 2000 by Summerwood Winery & Inn Inc. The structure was stripped down and completely remodeled, and the capacity for barrel storage was increased. What was once the cigar room is now a tropical-style gazebo complete with wicker chairs, palm trees, and bamboo curtains. Once inside the expansive tasting room, you can look through a wall of glass into the tank room, the fermentation room, and the barrel room beyond. The staff will tell you all about the activities going on in the winery and answer any questions. The tasting room has the friendly ambience of a lounge. In between tastings, you can settle in one of the comfortable oversized sofas and view the winemaking process on a wide-screen television.

From the tasting room, French doors open onto a brick deck landscaped with lavender bushes and overlooking the vineyards. At harvest time, this deck provides a view of grapes arriving at the crush pad. The winery is surrounded by a forty-five-acre vineyard, thirty-five of which are planted to Cabernet Sauvignon and Syrah. About 25 percent of the fifty-five-hundred-case annual production is made from estate grapes. The balance comes from purchased grapes from Paso's prime Westside vineyards, such as Denner, James Berry, Lock, Halter Ranch, and Jensen.

The focus at Summerwood is on Bordeaux and Rhône blends and some single varietals. All the wines are produced in small lots, some as low as a hundred cases. Experienced at working in France, Australia, and California, winemaker Scott Hawley applies old-world traditions to Summerwood's state-of-the-art facility. His goal is to bring in the best fruit possible and let it become wine with very little intervention. Besides single varietals, Hawley feels that he can show-case some wines best through blending. So, while he makes a single-varietal Viognier, he also creates Diosa Blanc, blending Viognier with Roussanne.

The percentage of varietal breakdown varies from year to year, depending on what nature provides in the vineyard. The red Diosa is a complex blend of Syrah, Mourvèdre, and Grenache, with layers of peppery spice, blueberry aromas, and a touch of plum. Like most Paso winemakers, Hawley gives his proprietary blend an individual touch. The Vin Rouge brings together the peppery notes of Zinfandel and the black fruit aromas of Syrah, with the addition of Cabernet Sauvignon and Cabernet Franc varying with each vintage. The flagship wine, Sentio, a Bordeaux blend of Cabernet Sauvignon, Merlot, and Cabernet Franc, comes packed with black fruit and bold tannins that give the wine aging potential.

Summerwood is dedicated to sustainable farming, incorporating insect borders and cover crops in between vine rows—such as planting California poppies that attract insects and clover that fixes nitrogen into the soil—beneficial for the vines' growth. Cover crops also compete with the vines, resulting in maximum flavor concentration in the grapes. The masses of wildflowers along the white fence attract beneficial insects that feed on pests. For example, ladybugs feed on harmful leafhopper larvae, eliminating the need for pesticides.

With its charming bed-and-breakfast, Summerwood is certainly a destination winery. The proprietors have created an environment where visitors can enjoy the wine-country experience for an extended stay. Nine luxuriously appointed rooms and suites are named after grape varietals. The beautifully landscaped grounds have meandering pathways for a pleasant stroll and arbors to relax under while taking in the serene vineyards. A hearty breakfast, afternoon appetizers, and homemade desserts are prepared by executive chef Kirk Sowell, whose menus are inspired by the local bounty and Summerwood's wines. The inn stages special wine-maker dinners, and Saturday-afternoon food-and-wine pairings are held on the winery's umbrella-shaded deck overlooking the Syrah and Cabernet Sauvignon vineyards.

102

SUMMERWOOD WINERY // 2175 Arbor Road, Paso Robles, CA 93446

T 805.227.1365
F 805.227.1366
E winery@summerwoodwine.com

www.summerwoodwine.com

ACCESS
From Highway 101, exit at Highway 46 West. Go west for 1 mile and turn right on Arbor Road.

Hours for visits and tastings:
10AM–5:30PM winter, 10AM–6PM summer. Closed on major holidays.

Wheelchair access.

TASTINGS & TOURS
Charge for tasting: $5.

Tours by appointment only.

Typical wines offered: Viognier, Cabernet Sauvignon, Syrah, Rhône blend, Bordeaux blend, and port.

Wine-related items for sale.

PICNICS & PROGRAMS
Picnic area open to the public. Picnic ingredients sold in tasting room.

Special events: Food-and-wine pairings on Saturdays, winemaker dinners, music and food during wine festival weekends. Check website for event calendar.

Wine club.

A visit to Tablas Creek allows you to taste the best of Rhône Valley wines without leaving the United States. The winery and vineyard operation is a joint venture between Jean-Pierre Perrin of Château de Beaucastel in Châteauneuf-du-Pape, southern France, and Robert Haas, founder of Vineyard Brands, a company known for importing fine wines from Europe. While Haas has been in business for more than half a century, the Perrin family has been making wine for even longer, since the early 1900s. The two families believed that California's climate would be well suited for growing Rhône varietals and were certain they could create a vineyard similar in style to the one in Châteauneuf-du-Pape.

The team's search took them from coastal Ventura County in the south to El Dorado Canyon near the Sierra Nevada foothills in the north. What they were looking for was climatic conditions similar to those in the Mediterranean region and high-pH soils like those in the Château de Beaucastel vineyard. They found both on the west side of Paso Robles. The property they settled on is loaded with white chunks of limestone shale, and the soil tested the same as that of Beaucastel. Hot days and nights cooled by the Pacific Ocean give the area a Rhône-like climate ideal for the grapes to mature fully while retaining their crisp acidity.

During their search for a site, Haas recalls that they were not impressed with the rootstock of the existing Rhône varietals in California. The old varieties in the state, such as Mourvèdre and Grenache, were around 150 years old. Since the growers had not taken good care of the vines, Haas and Perrin felt that their quality had degenerated. The partners decided to import vines from Beaucastel, including Mourvèdre, Grenache Noir, Syrah, Rousanne, Counoise, Viognier, Grenache Blanc, and Marsanne. This was no easy task. The cuttings had to go through a three-year quarantine, during which they were tested for viruses. The first imports arrived in 1990 and, over the years, were supplemented with new cuttings so the partners could reach their goal of planting 110 acres of vineyards.

A nursery with high-tech greenhouses and shade houses was constructed on-site in 1994. The newly arrived cuttings were grafted onto American rootstocks, which were gradually hardened off in sun and wind in preparation for planting in the vineyards. In 2004, the Tablas Creek team decided to outsource production and sales to the Sonoma-based Nova Vine Grapevine Nursery. The company collects the winery's discarded prunings every winter and does the grafting and marketing for Tablas Creek. Grapes from these vines have found their way into bottles of such noted Rhône producers as Garretson, Bonny Doon, Qupé, Ridge, Beckmen, Andrew Murray, and Zaca Mesa.

To fill the empty greenhouses, Tablas Creek collaborates with Windrose Farms to utilize the space. Owners Barbara and Bill Spencer now have two outlets: Windrose East, their fifty-acre farm in Templeton, and Windrose West, at Tablas Creek. At the winery, you can purchase their prized heirloom tomatoes and other organic fruits and vegetables from the produce stand.

Tablas Creek follows organic farming methods, harvests the fruit by hand, and uses native yeasts in fermentation. All the wines are made from grapes grown on the estate vineyard. At Tablas Creek, winemaker Neil Collins continues the centuries-old tradition of Châteauneuf-du-Pape by blending selected varietals that add complexity to the wine. A traditional Châteauneuf-du-Pape wine includes up to thirteen Rhône varietals. Tablas Creek's signature wine, Esprit de Beaucastel, is bottled as both a red and a white. The red is a blend of four traditional Rhône grapes: Mourvèdre, Syrah, Grenache Noir, and Counoise. The Blanc is a blend of Roussanne, Viognier, Grenache Blanc, and Marsanne. The winery also produces single varietals of Roussanne and Viognier. The wine-making team is experimenting with other varietals, such as Tannat, a red grape from the foothills of the Pyrenees Mountains in southwestern France. This powerful red is bold, with intense fruit and spice. Tannat is produced in limited quantities, so if you are in luck, the tasting room might have some bottles around.

Named after a creek that runs through the property, the winery is at fifteen hundred feet, above the winding Adelaida Road, and twelve miles from the Pacific Ocean. The curved driveway will bring you up the hill, where, surrounded by bursts of lavender and rosemary, you will be greeted by a road sign that reads "Domaine de Beaucastel, 9009 kilometers." The arrow on the sign points eastward in the direction of Tablas Creek's sister winery. At the tasting-room entrance sits a sample of the limestone rock found in the vineyards. Inside, creative ideas abound. The bar counter is a limestone slab atop a wrought-iron base, conceived by winemaker Collins and crafted by a local welder. The copper-topped rear counter comes from a barrel, and the wall shelves are made from barrel staves. Tables hold Provençal linens, tableware, assorted olive oils, and mustards. Don't miss the one-hour tour through the nursery, the vineyard, and the winery, concluding at the tasting room.

TABLAS CREEK VINEYARD // 9339 Adelaida Road, Paso Robles, CA 93446

T 805.237.1231
F 805.237.1314
E info@tablascreek.com

www.tablascreek.com

ACCESS
From Highway 101, take Highway 46 East exit. Travel west on 24th Street, which becomes Lake Nacimiento Road. Continue for 1.5 miles, turn left on Adelaida Road, and go 9.3 miles. Winery is on right past Vineyard Drive intersection.

Hours for visits and tastings:
10AM–5PM daily.
Closed on major holidays.

Wheelchair access.

TASTINGS & TOURS
Charge for tasting: $5; includes logo glass.

Tours, by appointment only, daily at 10:30AM and 2:30PM. No appointment required on festival weekends.

Typical wines offered: Rhône varietals and blends, including Côtes de Tablas and Côtes de Tablas Blanc, Esprit de Beaucastel and Esprit de Beaucastel Blanc, Rosé, Roussanne, Grenache Blanc, Syrah, and Mourvèdre.

Wine-related items for sale.

PICNICS & PROGRAMS
Picnic area open to public. No picnic ingredients sold in tasting room.

Special events: Monthly educational seminars on topics like organic farming, pruning and grafting, harvest, winemaking and blending; seasonal dinners and tastings. Check website for event calendar.

Wine club.

Windward Vineyard

OWNERS: **MARC GOLDBERG & MAGGIE D'AMBROSIA** // WINEMAKER: **MARC GOLDBERG**

Marc Goldberg has an intense passion for Pinot Noir. For the owner/winemaker of Windward Vineyard, the passion runs so deep that he produces this one varietal alone in his distinctive artisanal style. Along Highway 46 West, you might notice Windward's billboard bearing its "exclusively Pinot Noir" sign. As you turn left on Live Oak Road, Windward's prized Pinot Noir vineyards come into view along the winery's entrance. On the twenty-six-acre property, Goldberg and his wife, Maggie D'Ambrosia, planted fifteen acres to Pinot Noir vineyards in 1989. With careful attention to every minute detail, the team produces just seventeen hundred cases of handcrafted Pinot Noir per year.

A former Pennsylvania resident, Goldberg calls wine "a hobby and Pinot Noir my love." He first became infatuated with this varietal on his travels to Burgundy. After spending some time there, Marc and Maggie, former hospital administrators, decided to retire to a region where they could fulfill their dreams of making Burgundian-style wines. They found the perfect place on Paso's west side. In addition to the calcareous and well-drained rocky soils, the area receives cool ocean breezes that blow through the Templeton Gap, a break in the Santa Lucia Mountains. The resulting warm days and cool nights are ideal for Pinot Noir grapes.

Goldberg made several trips to Burgundy to learn the winemaking process and later honed his skills in Paso, working with Wild Horse Winery's veteran winemaker Ken Volk. Goldberg regards his style as more of an art than a science. "To me, the wines of Burgundy are an art form that is passed down through generations and depends more on wisdom gained from experience than on scientific intervention."

The Burgundian approach to winemaking begins in the vineyards by harvesting grapes that are not overripe. Otherwise, the wine would be too fruity, with unbalanced flavors. "We put in the bottle only what the vineyard gives us, so people will know from year to year that they are getting grapes from the same exact place," says Goldberg. Yet he admits that weather patterns can make a dramatic difference in the wine. He recalls the El Niño year of 1998, when a storm caused the grapes to be harvested in late October, six weeks later than usual. The long hang time–the period when the grapes are on the vine–and the late maturity impacted the wine. Although it expresses the characteristics of Windward, it does not have age potential, and will lose its flavors in less than twenty years. Conversely, the ideal warm weather will result in a perfect harvest, producing wines that will be worthy of cellaring for many years.

The winery is housed in a seventy-year-old barn that has retained its aged patina. "When we bought the place," Goldberg recalls, "it had no walls, just four thousand square feet of space filled with old cars and tractors." The couple rebuilt it one section at a time, finally finishing the tasting room in 2002. The interior, painted in a faux finish by local artist Mike Dwallabee, evokes a country French mood. A wrought-iron grapevine winds up a pole at the entrance, and a large ceramic sculpture of the Windward logo tops the building. For the logo, Paso artist David Butz fused the image of the wind god, who resembles Goldberg, blowing out a fierce puff. The owners chose the name because of the coastal winds that blow in from nearby Templeton Gap.

Inside the tasting room, impressionistic artworks by James Paul Brown of Santa Barbara hang on a wall. A spiral stairway leads to a mezzanine-level cubicle that serves as the couple's office. A barrel room adjacent to the tasting room holds just a hundred barrels. Tours of the winery and vineyards can be arranged by appointment. Depending on the level of your interest, you might even be given an impromptu barrel tasting.

Since the winery offers just one varietal, you will experience a vertical tasting (the same wine but different years) of three vintages of Pinot Noir, wines that are lush and velvety, with wild strawberry aromas. You'll notice that Windward bottles bear the word *Monopole*, a Burgundian designation signifying sole ownership of a vineyard and wine made only from grapes grown in that particular vineyard. Being a purist about Pinot Noir from his estate vineyards, Goldberg chooses to add Monopole to his label instead of using the customary term "estate grown" or stating the designated vineyard, as is common on American bottles. He argues that some California wineries that label their bottles estate grown or single-vineyard designates may actually include a small percentage of grapes from multiple vineyards, or other varietals such as some Syrah.

Windward has a reputation not only for excellent wines but also for food and wine programs. The French Connection dinner, staged two to three times a year, is a side-by-side tasting of Windward wines and Grand Cru Burgundies of similar vintages. Another popular event is the Pinot and Paella Cook-Off, started by Goldberg to benefit local youth charities. Several local chefs prepare their versions of paella, which are then paired with Pinots by an equal number of wineries. The event takes place at the June festival in Templeton's Community Park.

To fully enjoy Windward's seductive Pinot Noir, savor it on the shaded, ivy-covered deck, overlooking rows of well-tended vineyards.

WINDWARD VINEYARD // 1380 Live Oak Road, Paso Robles, CA 93446

T 805.239.2565
F 805.239.4005
E Maggie@windwardvineyard.com

www.windwardvineyard.com

ACCESS
From Highway 101, take Highway 46 West exit. Drive west for 1 mile, turn right on Arbor Road, go .25 mile to Live Oak Road, and turn left. Winery is on right.

Hours for visits and tastings:
11AM – 5AM daily.

TASTINGS & TOURS
Charge for tasting: $5 includes regular glass; $10 includes engraved Riedel glass.

Tours by appointment only.

Typical wine offered: Pinot Noir.

Wine-related items for sale.

PICNICS & PROGRAMS
Picnic area open to public. No picnic ingredients sold in tasting room.

Special events: Participation in all Paso Robles appellation events. Check website for event calendar.

Wine club.

Resources

SANTA BARBARA COUNTY

[note]: All resources are in the 805 telephone area code unless otherwise given.

HISTORICAL SITES

Casa del Herrero
1387 East Valley Road
Montecito 93108
T 565.5653
www.casadelherrero.com

La Purisima Mission
2295 Purisima Road
Lompoc 93436
T 733.3713
www.lapurisimamission.org

Mission Santa Barbara
2201 Laguna Street
Santa Barbara 93105
T 682.4149
www.sbmission.org/history.shtml

Mission Santa Ines
1760 Mission Drive
Solvang 93464
T 688.4815
www.missionsantaines.org

Santa Barbara Historical Society
136 East De La Guerra Street
Santa Barbara 93101
T 966.1601
www.santabarbaramuseum.com

CERTIFIED FARMERS' MARKETS

Carpinteria
800 block of Linden Avenue
Thursday 3–6PM (winter)
4–7PM (summer)

Goleta
Camino Real Marketplace
7004 Marketplace Drive
Sunday 10AM–2PM

Goleta
5700 Calle Real
Thursday 3–6PM

Lompoc
Corner of Ocean Avenue and I Street
Friday 2–6PM

Montecito
1100–1200 Coast Village Road
Friday 8–11:15AM

Santa Barbara
La Cumbre Plaza
121 South Hope Avenue
(inside shopping center)
Wednesday 1–5PM (winter)
2–6PM (summer)

Santa Barbara Downtown
Corner of Santa Barbara and Cota Streets
Saturday 8:30AM–12:30PM

Santa Barbara Old Town
500–600 State Street
Tuesday 3–6:30PM (winter)
4–7:30PM (summer)

Santa Maria
Central City Farmers' Market
Oak Knoll South,
corner of Bradley Road
and Clark Avenue
Tuesday 10AM–1PM

Santa Maria
Town Center West
Broadway and Main Street
Wednesday 12:15–4PM

Solvang Village
Copenhagen Drive and First Street
Wednesday 3–6PM (winter)
4–7PM (summer)

WINE & CULINARY EDUCATION

Allan Hancock College
800 South College
Santa Maria
T 922.6966, ext. 3760
www.hancockcollege.edu

Chef Isabelle Alexandre at Citronelle
Citronelle at Santa Barbara Inn
901 East Cabrillo Boulevard
Santa Barbara
T 963.0111
www.santabarbarainn.com

Chef Jean-Philippe Sitbon
2017 El Camino de la Luz
Santa Barbara
T 966.4574
www.atyourservicechef.com

Chef Leonardo Curti of Trattoria Grappolo
Santa Ynez
T 688.6899 or 350.1832
www.trattoriagrappolo.com

Chef Michael Hutchings
Carpinteria
T 451.6738
www.chefmichaelhutchings.com

Chef's Touch
1555 Mission Drive
Solvang
T 686.1040

Cook & Ladder, Coleman Farms, & Shepherd Farms
3280 Calzada Avenue
Santa Ynez
T 688.4711
www.cookandladder.com

El Rancho Marketplace
2886 Mission Drive
Solvang
T 688.4300
www.elranchomarket.com

Hotel Mar Monte
1111 East Cabrillo Boulevard
Santa Barbara
T 730.1111

McKeon-Phillips Winery
2115 South Blosser, Ste. 114
Santa Maria
T 928.3025
www.mckeonphillipswinery.com

Montecito Country Kitchen
T 569.1021
www.montecitocountrykitchen.com

MAJOR WINE & FOOD EVENTS CALENDAR

Ongoing
Santa Barbara Museum of Natural History's Food Series
2559 Puesta del Sol Road
Santa Barbara
T 682.4711, ext. 117
www.sbnature.org

March
Taste of Solvang
Solvang
T 688.6144

110

March & April

Santa Barbara Wine Futures Tasting
Wine Cask Restaurant
813 Anacapa Street
Santa Barbara
T 966.9463
www.winecask.com

April

Santa Barbara County Vintners' Festival
Firestone Meadow
Foxen Canyon Road
Los Olivos
T 688.0881
www.sbcountywines.com

Rideau Vintners' Weekend Open House
Rideau Vineyards
1562 Alamo Pintado Road
Solvang
T 688.0717
www.rideauvineyard.com

Santa Maria Strawberry Festival
937 South Thornburg
Santa Maria
T 925.8824
www.santamariafairpark.com

May

Downtown Art & Wine Tour
Downtown Santa Barbara
T 962.2098
www.santabarbaradowntown.com

June

Lompoc's Annual Flower Festival
T 735.8511
www.flowerfestival.org

July

Touring & Tasting's Annual California Wine Festival
Chase Palm Park
Santa Barbara
T 850.4370
www.touringandtasting.com

September

Taste of the Town
Riviera Park and Gardens
Santa Barbara
T 892.5556

Old Town Harvest Festival
Santa Barbara Old Town
T 962.2098
www.santabarbaradowntown.com

California Organic Festival
Alameda and Alice Keck Parks
Santa Barbara
T 965.4497
www.organicfestival.com

October

Celebration of Harvest
Rancho Sisquoc Winery
6600 Foxen Canyon Road
Santa Maria
T 688.0881
www.sbcountywines.com

Autumn Arts, Grapes & Grains Festival
McClelland Street
Santa Maria
T 925.2403
www.santamaria.com

Santa Barbara Harbor & Seafood Festival
Santa Barbara Harbor
T 564.5531

California Lemon Festival in Goleta
Girsh Park
Goleta
T 646.5382
www.goletavalley.com

California Avocado Festival
Downtown Carpinteria
T 684.0038
www.avofest.com

Real Men Cook
Monty and Pat Roberts' Flag Is Up Farms
Solvang
T 688.9533

December

Elizabethan Christmas in the Caves
Cottonwood Canyon Winery
3940 Dominion Road
Santa Maria
T 937.9063

TOUR COMPANIES

Adventurous Outdoor Excursions
T 899.2929
www.adventours.com

American International Transportation
T 643.5466 or 334.5466
www.aitslimo.com

Breakaway Tours & Event Planning
T 783.2929 or 799.7657
www.breakaway.tours.com

Cloud Climbers Jeep Tours
T 965.6654
www.ccjeeps.com

Personal Tours, Ltd.
T 685.0552
www.personaltoursltd.com

Riviera Tours
T 899.2266
www.rivieratours.com

Stardust Cruises
T 938.0018
www.stardustcruises.com

TravelValet of Santa Barbara
T 963.9263
E travelvalet@att.net

Wine'edVentures
T 965.9463
www.welovewines.com

VISITORS BUREAUS & CHAMBERS OF COMMERCE

Buellton Visitors' Bureau & Chamber of Commerce
T 688.STAY or 800.324.3800
www.buellton.org

Lompoc Valley Chamber of Commerce
T 736.4567
www.lompoc.com

Santa Barbara Chamber of Commerce
T 965.3023
www.sbchamber.org

Santa Barbara County Vintners' Association
T 688.0881 or 800.218.0881
www.sbcountywines.com

Santa Maria Valley Chamber of Commerce and Visitor & Convention Bureau
T 925.2403 or 800.331.3779
www.santamaria.com

Santa Ynez Valley Visitors' Association
T 800.742.2843
www.syvva.com

Solvang Conference & Visitors Bureau
T 688.6144 or 800.468.6765
www.solvangusa.com

Resources

SAN LUIS OBISPO COUNTY

[note]: All resources are in the 805 telephone area code unless otherwise given.

HISTORICAL SITES

Carnegie Historic Library Museum
1000 Spring Street
Paso Robles 93446
T 238.4996
www.californiahistoricalsociety.org

Estrella Warbirds Museum
4251 Dry Creek Road
Paso Robles 93446
T 227.0440
www.ewarbirds.org

Hearst Castle
750 Hearst Castle Road
San Simeon 93452
T 800.444.4445
www.hearstcastle.com

Mission San Miguel Arcangel
775 Mission Street
San Miguel 93451
T 467.3256
www.missionsanmiguel.org

Pioneer Museum
2010 Riverside Avenue
Paso Robles 93447
T 239.4556

Rios-Caledonia Adobe
700 Mission Street
San Miguel 93451
T 467.3357
www.slocountyparks.com

CERTIFIED FARMERS' MARKETS

Arroyo Grande Farmers' Market
Oak Park Plaza
Arroyo Grande
Wednesday 9–11AM

Arroyo Grande Farmers' Market
City Hall parking lot
215 East Branch Street
Arroyo Grande
Saturday 12–2:30PM

Atascadero Farmers' Market
El Camino Real and Morro Road
Atascadero
Wednesday 3–6PM

Cambria Farmers' Market
West Main Street next to Vet's Hall
Cambria
Friday 2:30–5PM (winter)
2:30–5:30PM (summer)

Cayucos Farmers' Market
Veterans Hall Parking Lot
Cayucos
Friday 9AM–noon (May–Nov.)

County Farm and Craft Market
Paso Robles City Park
Saturday 8AM–noon

Country Farm and Craft Market
Mission Street (between 10th and 11th)
San Miguel
Sunday 10AM–2PM

Fishermen and Farmers' Market
Harbor and Morro Streets
Morro Bay
Saturday 3–6PM

Main Street Market & Music
Between Entrada and West Mall
Atascadero
Wednesday 6–9PM

Morro Bay Farmers' Market
Spencer's Market, 2650 Main Street
Morro Bay
Thursday 3–5PM

Paso Robles Farmers' Market
Paso Robles City Park
940 Park Street
Tuesday 10AM–1PM

San Luis Obispo Farmers' Market
Higuera Street from Nipomo to Osos Street
San Luis Obispo
Thursday 6–9PM

San Luis Obispo Farmers' Market
Madonna Road near Promenade Shopping Center
San Luis Obispo
Saturday 8–10:30AM

Templeton Farmers' Market
City Park at Sixth and Crocker Streets
Templeton
Saturday 9AM–12:30PM

WINE & CULINARY EDUCATION

AgAdventures
545 Main Street, Ste. B1
Morro Bay
T 800.918.1999
www.agadventures.org

Paso Robles Wine University
1232 Park Street
Paso Robles 93446
T 239.8463
www.pasowine.com

WineYard at Steinbeck Vineyards
5940 Union Road
Paso Robles 93446
T 238.1854
www.thevineyard.com

MAJOR WINE & FOOD EVENTS CALENDAR

January
Esprit du Vin
(Wineries of 46 East)
T 226.7133
www.pasowine46east.com

March
Paso Robles Zinfandel Festival
California Mid-State Fair Grounds
2198 Riverside Avenue
Paso Robles
T 239.8463
www.pasowine.com

May
Paso Robles Wine Festival
Paso Robles City Park
T 239.8463
www.pasowine.com

Hospice du Rhône
California Mid-State Fair Grounds
2198 Riverside Avenue
Paso Robles
T 784.9543
www.hospicedurhone.com

August
Winemaker's Invitational Barbecue Cook-Off and Wine Tasting
Paso Robles Hot Springs and Spa
T 238.0506
www.pasoroblesrotary.org

October

Basil Harvest Festival
Sycamore Farms
T 238.5288
www.sycamorefarms.com

Paso Robles Harvest Wine Tour
(75 wineries in Paso Robles)
T 239.8463
www.pasowine.com

TOUR COMPANIES

At Your Service Limousine
T 239.8785
www.tcsn.net/ays

Breakaway Tours & Events Planning
T 783.2929
www.breakaway-tours.com

Central Coast Wine Tours
T 866.717.2298
www.ccwt.net

The Grapevine Wine Country Shuttle
T 239.4747
www.pasorobles.gogrape.com

North American Jet Charter
T 238.1027
www.flynajc.com

Paso Robles Wine Train
T 949.707.0707
www.pasowinetrain.com

Paso Robles Wine Trolley & Tour Company
T 296.9633
www.pasowinetrolley.com

Silverado Stages
T 545.8400
www.silveradotours.com

Sinton Helicopters
T 238.4037
www.sintonhelicopters.com

Sultan's Limousine Service
T 466.3167
www.sultanslimo.com

The Wine Wrangler
T 238.5700
www.thewinewrangler.com

VISITORS BUREAUS & CHAMBERS OF COMMERCE

Arroyo Grande Chamber of Commerce
T 489.1488
www.arroyograndecc.com

Paso Robles Chamber of Commerce and Visitors & Conference Bureau
T 238.0506
www.Go2Paso.com

Paso Robles Wine Country Alliance
T 239.8463
www.pasowine.com

San Luis Obispo Chamber of Commerce
T 781.2777
www.slochamber.org

San Luis Obispo County Visitors & Conference Bureau
T 541.8000
www.sanluisobispocounty.com

San Simeon Chamber of Commerce
T 927.3500 or 800.342.5613
www.sansimeonchamber.com

Templeton Chamber of Commerce
T 434.1789
www.templetonchamber.com

FARM STAYS
(for overnight and day visits)

Fair Oaks Ranch
7365 Adelaida Road
Paso Robles
T 238.3811
www.forbeef.com

Hollyhock Farms
200 Hollyhock Lane
Templeton
T 239.4713
www.hollyhock-farm.com

Lazy Arrow Outdoor Adventures
9330 Camatta Creek Road
Santa Margarita
T 238.7324
www.lazyarrow.com

Starr Ranch
9320 Chimney Rock Road
Paso Robles
T 227.0144
www.starr-ranch.com

Windrose Farms
5750 El Pharo Drive
Paso Robles
T 239.3757
www.windrosefarm.org

Work Family Guest Ranch
75893 Ranchita Canyon
San Miguel
T 467.3362
www.workranch.com

FARMS
(day visits only)

Jack Creek Farms
5000 Highway 46 West
Templeton
T 238.3799
www.jackcreekfarms.com
Open seasonally
July–September: weekends only 10AM–6PM
October: daily 10AM–6PM (10AM–5PM after daylight savings time ends)

Mt. Olive Organic Farm
3445 Adelaida Road
Paso Robles
T 237.0147
www.mtoliveco.com
Open Thursday–Sunday
November–April: 10AM–5PM
March–October: 10AM–7PM

Willow Creek Ranch
8530 Vineyard Drive
Paso Robles
T 227.0186
www.pasolivo.com
Friday–Sunday 11AM–5PM
Other days by appointment.

Directory of Central Coast Wineries

Alexander & Wayne
2923 Grand Avenue
Los Olivos, CA 93441
T 805.688.9665
www.alexanderandwayne.com

Andrew Murray Vineyards
2901 Grand Avenue
Los Olivos, CA 93441
T 805.693.9644
www.andrewmurrayvineyards.com

**Artiste Winery
& Tasting Studio**
3569 Sagunto Street
Santa Ynez, CA 93460
T 805.686.2626
www.artiste.com

**Au Bon Climat/
Cold Heaven Cellars**
3631 Sagunto Street
Santa Ynez, CA 93460
T 805.688.8688
www.aubonclimat.com

Babcock Winery & Vineyard
5175 E. Highway 246
Lompoc, CA 93013
T 805.736.1455
www.babcockwinery.com

Beckmen Vineyards
2670 Ontiveros Road
Los Olivos, CA 93441
T 805.688.8664
www.beckmenvineyards.com

**Bedford Thompson Winery
& Vineyard**
448 Bell Street
Los Alamos, CA 93440
T 805.344.2107
www.bedfordthompsonwinery.com

Bernat Vineyards & Winery
2879 Grand Avenue
Los Olivos, CA 93441
T 805.688.7265 ext. 206
www.santabarbarawine.com

Blackjack Ranch
2205 Alamo Pintado Road
Solvang, CA 93463
T 805.686.9922
Email: bjranch@aol.com

Brander Vineyard
154 Roblar Avenue
Santa Ynez, CA 93460
T 805.688.2455
www.brander.com

Bridlewood Winery
3555 Roblar Avenue
Santa Ynez, CA 93460
T 805.688.9000
www.bridlewoodwinery.com

Brophy Clark Cellars
2905 Grand Avenue
Los Olivos, CA 93441
T 805.929.4830
www.brophyclarkcellars.com

**Buttonwood Farm Winery
& Vineyard**
1500 Alamo Pintado Road
Solvang, CA 93463
T 805.688.3032
www.buttonwoodwinery.com

**Byron Vineyard
& Winery**
(by appointment only)
5250 Tepusquet Road
Santa Maria, CA 93454
T 805.934.4770
www.byronwines.com

**Cambria Estate Vineyard
& Winery**
5475 Chardonnay Lane
Santa Maria, CA 93454
T 805.937.9463
www.cambriawines.com

**Carhartt Vineyard
& Winery**
1691 Alamo Pintado Road
Solvang, CA 93463
T 805.688.0685
www.carharttvineyard.com

Carina Cellars
2900 Grand Avenue
Los Olivos, CA 93441
T 805.688.2459
www.carinacellars.com

**Casa Cassara Winery
& Vineyard**
1661 Mission Drive
Solvang, CA 93463
T 805.688.5159
www.casacassarawinery.com

Cellar 205 & Marketplace
205 Anacapa Street
Santa Barbara, CA 93101
T 805.962.5857
www.cellar205.com

Consilience
2933 Grand Avenue
Los Olivos, CA 93441
T 805.691.1020
www.consiliencewines.com

**Cottonwood Canyon Vineyard
& Winery**
3940 Dominion Road
Santa Maria, CA 93454
T 805.937.8463
www.cottonwoodcanyon.com

Curtis Winery
5249 Foxen Canyon Road
Los Olivos, CA 93441
T 805.686.8999
www.curtiswinery.com

Daniel Gehrs Wines
2939 Grand Avenue
Los Olivos, CA 93441
T 805.275.8138
www.dgwines.com

Epiphany Cellars
2963 Grand Avenue
Los Olivos, CA 93441
T 805.686.2424
www.epiphanycellars.com

**Fess Parker Winery
& Vineyard**
6200 Foxen Canyon Road
Los Olivos, CA 93441
T 805.688.1545
www.fessparker.com

Firestone Vineyard
5000 Zaca Station Road
Los Olivos, CA 93441
T 805.688.3940
www.firestonewine.com

**Foley Estate Vineyard
& Winery**
6121 East Highway 246
Lompoc, CA 93013
T 805.688.8554
www.foleywines.com

Foxen Vineyard
7200 Foxen Canyon Road
Santa Maria, CA 93454
T 805.937.4251
www.foxenvineyard.com

Gainey Vineyard
3950 East Highway 246
Santa Ynez, CA 93460
T 805.688.0558
www.gaineyvineyard.com

Hitching Post Wines
406 East Highway 246
Buellton, CA 93427
T 805.688.0676
www.hitchingpostwines.com

Huber Cellars
1539 Mission Drive, Unit A
Solvang, CA 93463
T 805.686.9323
www.hubercellars.com

Jaffurs Wine Cellars
819 East Montecito Street
Santa Barbara, CA 93103
T 805.962.7003
www.jaffurswine.com

Kalyra Winery
343 North Refugio Road
Santa Ynez, CA 93460
T 805.693.8864
www.kalyrawinery.com

Koehler Winery
5360 Foxen Canyon Road
Los Olivos, CA 93441
T 805.693.8384
www.koehlerwinery.com

Lafond Winery
6855 Santa Rosa Road
Buellton, CA 93427
T 805.688.7921
www.lafondwinery.com

Lincourt Vineyards
1711 Alamo Pintado Road
Solvang, CA 93463
T 805.688.8554
www.lincourtwines.com

Longoria Wines
2935 Grand Avenue
Los Olivos, CA 93441
T 805.688.0305
www.longoriawine.com

Lucas & Lewellen Vineyards
1645 Copenhagen Drive
Solvang, CA 93463
T 805.686.9336
www.llwine.com

Mandolina
1665 Copenhagen Drive
Solvang, CA 93463
T 805.686.5506
www.mandolina.com

Margerum Wine Company
813 Anacapa Street
Santa Barbara, CA 93103
T 805.966.9463
www.margerumwinecompany.com

McKeon-Phillips
2115 South Blosser Road
Santa Maria, CA 93458
T 805.928.3025
www.mckeonphillipswinery.com

Melville Winery
5185 East Highway 246
Lompoc, CA 93436
T 805.735.5310
www.melvillewinery.com

Mosby Winery & Vineyards
9496 Santa Rosa Road
Buellton, CA 93427
T 805.688.2415 or 800.70.MOSBY
www.mosbywines.com

Oak Savanna Vineyard
2901 Grand Avenue
Los Olivos, CA 93441
T 805.693.9644
www.oaksavannawine.com

Presidio Winery
1603 Copenhagen
Solvang, CA 93436
T 805.693.8585
www.presidiowinery.com

Rancho Sisquoc Winery
6600 Foxen Canyon Road
Santa Maria, CA 93454
T 805.934.4332
www.ranchosisquoc.com

Rideau Vineyard
1562 Alamo Pintado Road
Solvang, CA 93463
T 805.688.0717
www.rideauvineyard.com

Royal Oaks Winery
1651 Copenhagen Drive
Solvang, CA 93463
T 805.693.1740
www.royaloakswinery.com

Rusack Vineyards
1819 Ballard Canyon Road
Solvang, CA 93463
T 805.688.1278
www.rusackvineyards.com

Sanford Winery & Vineyards
7250 Santa Rosa Road
Buellton, CA 93427
T 805.688.3300 or 800.426.9463
www.sanfordwinery.com

Santa Barbara Winery
202 Anacapa Street
Santa Barbara, CA 93101
T 805.963.3633 or 800.225.3633
www.sbwinery.com

**Shoestring Vineyards
& Winery**
800 East Highway 246
Solvang, CA 93460
T 805.693.8612
www.shoestringwinery.com

Stolpman Vineyards
1659 Copenhagen Drive
Solvang, CA 93463
T 805.688.0400
www.stolpmanvineyards.com

Summerland Winery
2330 Lillie Avenue
Summerland, CA 93067
T 805.565.WINE
www.summerlandwine.com

Sunstone Vineyards & Winery
125 Refugio Road
Santa Ynez, CA 93460
T 805.688.9463 or 800.313.9463
www.sunstonewinery.com

Tantara Winery
(by appt. only)
4747 Ontiveros Lane
Santa Maria, CA 93454
T 805.938.5051
www.tantarawinery.com

Zaca Mesa Winery
6905 Foxen Canyon Road
Los Olivos, CA 93441
T 805.688.9339, 800.350.7972
www.zacamesa.com

SAN LUIS OBISPO COUNTY

PASO ROBLES

Adelaida Cellars
5805 Adelaida Road
Paso Robles, CA 93446
T 805.239.8980
www.adelaida.com

AJB Vineyards
3280 Township Road
Paso Robles, CA 93446
T 805.239.9432
www.ajbvineyards.com

Anglim Winery
740 Pine Street
Paso Robles, CA 93446
T 805.227.6813
www.anglimwinery.com

Arroyo Robles Winery
390 San Marcos Road
Paso Robles, CA 93446
T 805.759.WINE
www.arroyorobles.com

Bella Luna Winery
1850 Templeton Road
Templeton, CA 93465
T 805.434.5477
www.bellalunawine.com

Bianchi Vineyards
3380 Branch Road
Paso Robles, CA 93446
T 805.226.9922
www.bianchiwine.com

Calcareous Vineyards
1606 Windstar Court
Paso Robles, CA 93446
T 805.239.0289
www.calcareous.com

Caparone Winery
2280 San Marcos Road
Paso Robles, CA 93446
T 805.467.3827
www.caparone.com

**Carmody McKnight
Estate Wines**
11240 Chimney Rock Road
Paso Robles, CA 93446
T 805.238.9392
www.carmodymcknight.com

Casa de Caballos Vineyards
2225 Raymond Avenue
Templeton, CA 93465
T 805.434.1687
www.casadecaballos.com

Cass Winery
7350 Linne Road
Paso Robles, CA 93446
T 805.239.1730
www.casswines.com

Castoro Cellars
1315 No. Bethel Road
Templeton, CA 93465
T 805.DAM-FINE
www.castorocellars.com

Changala Winery
3760 Willow Creek Road
Paso Robles, CA 93446
T 805.238.0421
www.changalawinery.com

Château de Deighton
2515 Lara Lane
Oceano, CA 93445
T 805.489.0979
www.ChateauDeDeighton.com

Chateau Margene
4385 La Panza
Creston, CA 93432
T 805.238.2321
www.chateaumargene.com

Chumeia Vineyards
8331 Highway 46 East
Paso Robles, CA 93446
T 805.226.0102
www.chumeiavineyards.com

Clautiere Vineyard
1020 Penman Springs Road
Paso Robles, CA 93446
T 805.237.3789
www.clautiere.com

Clayhouse Vineyard
179 Niblick Road, PMB 332
Paso Robles, CA 93446
T 805.239.8989
www.clayhousewines.com

Coastal Vintners
2323 Tuley Court, Suite 120-D
Paso Robles, CA 93446
T 805.226.8022
www.coastalvintners.com

Dark Star Cellars
2985 Anderson Road
Paso Robles, CA 93446
T 805.237.2389
www.darkstarcellars.com

Denner Vineyards & Winery
5414 Vineyard Drive
Paso Robles, CA 93446
T 805.239.4287
www.dennervineyards.com

**Doce Robles Winery
& Vineyard**
2023 Twelve Oaks Drive
Paso Robles, CA 93446
T 805.227.4766
E docerobleswinery@tcsn.net

Dover Canyon Winery
4520 Vineyard Drive
Paso Robles, CA 93446
T 805.237.0101
www.dovercanyon.com

Dunning Vineyards
1953 Niderer Road
Paso Robles, CA 93446
T 805.238.4763
www.dunningvineyards.com

Eagle Castle Winery
2428 Royal Court
Paso Robles, CA 93446
T 805.227.1428
www.eaglecastlewinery.com

Eberle Winery
3810 Highway 46 East
Paso Robles, CA 93446
T 805.238.9607
www.eberlewinery.com

EOS Estate at Arciero
5625 Highway 46 East
Paso Robles, CA 93446
T 805.239.2562
www.eosvintage.com

Directory of Central Coast Wineries

PASO ROBLES, continued

Four Vines Winery
3750 Highway 46 West
Templeton, CA 93465
T 805.237.0055
www.fourvines.com

Fratelli Perata
1595 Arbor Road
Paso Robles, CA 93446
T 805.238.2809
www.fratelliperata.com

Gelfand Vineyards
5530 Dresser Ranch Place
Paso Robles, CA 93446
T 805.239.5808
www.gelfandvineyards.com

Grey Wolf Cellars
2174 Highway 46 West
Paso Robles, CA 93446
T 805.237.0771
www.grey-wolfcellars.com

Halter Ranch Vineyard
8910 Adelaida Road
Paso Robles, CA 93446
T 805.226.9455
www.halterranch.com

Hansen Vineyard
5575 El Pomar
Templeton, CA 93465
T 805.239.8412

Harmony Cellars
3255 Harmony Valley Road
Harmony, CA 93435
T 805.927.1625
www.harmonycellars.com

Hidden Mountain Ranch
2740 Hidden Mountain Road
Paso Robles, CA 93446
T 805.238.7143

Hug Cellars
2323 Tuley Court, Ste. 120D
Paso Robles, CA 93446
T 805.828.5906
www.hugcellars.com

Hunt Cellars
2875 Oakdale Road
Paso Robles, CA 93446
T 805.237.1600
www.huntwinecellars.com

J. Lohr Vineyards & Wines
6169 Airport Road
Paso Robles, CA 93446
T 805.239.8900
www.jlohr.com

Jack Creek Cellars
5265 Jack Creek Road
Templeton, CA 93465
T 805.226.8283
www.jackcreekcellars.com

JanKris Winery
1266 North Bethel Road
Templeton, CA 93465
T 805.434.0319
www.jankriswinery.com

Justin Vineyards & Winery
11680 Chimney Rock Road
Paso Robles, CA 93446
T 805.237.4149
www.JUSTINwine.com

L'Aventure Winery
2815 Live Oak Road
Paso Robles, CA 93446
T 805.227.1588
www.aventurewine.com

Linne Calodo Cellars
3845 Oakdale Road
Paso Robles, CA 93446
T 805.227.0797

**Locatelli Vineyards
& Winery**
8585 Cross Canyons Road
San Miguel, CA 93451
T 805.467.0067
www.locatelliwinery.com

Madison Cellars
1761 Ramada Drive
Paso Robles, CA 93446
T 805.237.7544
www.madisoncellars.com

Maloy O'Neill Vineyards
5725 Union Road
Paso Robles, CA 93446
T 805.238.7320
www.maloyoneill.com

Martin & Weyrich Winery
2610 Buena Vista Drive
Paso Robles, CA 93446
T 805.238.2520
www.martinweyrich.com

Mastantuono Winery
2720 Oak View
Templeton, CA 93465
T 805.238.0676
www.mastantuonowinery.com

McClean Vineyards
4491 South El Pomar Drive
Templeton, CA 93465
T 805.237.2441
www.mccleanvineyard.com

Meridian Vineyards
7000 Highway 46 East
Paso Robles, CA 93446
T 805.226.7133
www.meridianvineyards.com

Midnight Cellars
2925 Anderson Road
Paso Robles, CA 93446
T 805.239.8904
www.midnightcellars.com

Minassian–Young Vineyards
4045 Peachy Canyon Road
Paso Robles, CA 93446
T 805.238.7571

Nadeau Family Vintners
3860 Peachy Canyon Road
Paso Robles, CA 93447
T 805.239.3574
www.nadeaufamilyvintners.com

Niner Wine Estates
1322 Morro Street
San Luis Obispo, CA 93401
T 805.239.2233
www.ninerwine.com

Norman Vineyards
7450 Vineyard Drive
Paso Robles, CA 93446
T 805.237.0138
www.normanvineyards.com

Opolo Vineyards
7110 Vineyard Drive
Paso Robles, CA 93446
T 805.238.9593
www.opolo.com

Peachy Canyon Winery
2025 Nacimiento Lake Road
Paso Robles, CA 93446
T 805.239.1918
www.peachycanyon.com

Penman Springs Vineyard
1985 Penman Springs Road
Paso Robles, CA 93446
T 805.237.7959
www.penmansprings.com

Perbacco Cellars
1850 Calle Joaquin
San Luis Obispo, CA 93405
T 805.787.0485
www.perbaccocellars.com

Pipestone Vineyards
2040 Niderer Road
Paso Robles, CA 93446
T 805.227.6385
www.pipestonevineyards.com

Pretty-Smith Vineyards
13350 River Road
San Miguel, CA 93451
T 805.467.3104
www.prettysmith.com

Rabbit Ridge Vineyards
1172 San Marcos Road
Paso Robles, CA 93446
T 805.467.3331
www.rabbitridgewinery.com

Rainbows End Vineyard
8535 Mission Street
San Miguel, CA 93451
T 805.467.0044
www.rainbowsendvineyard.com

Rio Seco Vineyard & Winery
4295 Union Road
Paso Robles, CA 93446
T 805.237.8884
www.riosecowine.com

Riverstar Ranch & Vineyards
36 North Ocean Avenue
Cayucos, CA 93430
T 805.995.3741
www.riverstarvineyards.com

RN Estate
7986 North River Road
Paso Robles, CA 93446
T 805.467.3106
www.rnestate.com

Robert Hall Winery
3443 Mill Road
Paso Robles, CA 93446
T 805.239.1616
www.roberthallwinery.com

Rotta Winery
3750 Highway 46 West
Templeton, CA 93465
T 805.237.0510
www.rottawinery.com

San Marcos Creek Vineyard
7750 North Highway 101
Paso Robles, CA 93446
T 805.467.2670
www.sanmarcoscreekvineyard.com

Silver Horse Vineyards
2995 Pleasant Road
San Miguel, CA 93451
T 805.467.9463
www.silverhorse.com

Silver Stone
2041 Summit Drive
Paso Robles, CA 93446
T 805.227.6434
www.silverstonewines.com

Skyhawk Lane
211 Oro Drive
Arroyo Grande, CA 93420
T 805.474.4277
www.SkyhawkLane.com

Stacked Stone Cellars
1525 Peachy Canyon Road
Paso Robles, CA 93446
T 805.238.7872
www.stackedstone.com

Stephen's Cellar & Vineyard
7575 York Mountain Road
Templeton, CA 93465
T 805.238.2412
www.stephenscellar.com

Still Waters Vineyards
2750 Old Grove Lane
Paso Robles, CA 93446
T 805.237.9231
www.stillwatersvineyards.com

Summerwood Winery
2175 Arbor Road
Paso Robles, CA 93446
T 805.227.1365
www.summerwoodwine.com

Sylvester Winery
5115 Buena Vista Drive
Paso Robles, CA 93446
T 805.227.4000
www.sylvesterwinery.com

Tablas Creek Vineyard
9339 Adelaida Road
Paso Robles, CA 93446
T 805.237.1231
www.tablascreek.com

Tobin James
8950 Union Road
Paso Robles, CA 93446
T 805.239.2204
www.tobinjames.com

Turley Wine Cellars
2900 Vineyard Drive
Templeton, CA 93465
T 805.434.1030
www.turleywinecellars.com

Victor Hugo Vineyard & Winery
2850 El Pomar Drive
Templeton, CA 93465
T 805.434.1128
www.victorhugowinery.com

Villicana Winery
2725 Adelaida Road
Paso Robles, CA 93446
T 805.239.9456
www.villicanawinery.com

Vina Robles
Highway 46 East at Mill Road
Paso Robles, CA 93447
T 805.227.4812
www.vinarobles.com

Vista Del Rey Vineyards
7340 Drake Road
Paso Robles, CA 93446
F 805.467.2138

Wild Coyote
3775 Adelaida Road
Paso Robles, CA 93446
T 805.610.1311
www.wildcoyote.biz

Wild Horse Winery & Vineyard
1437 Wild Horse Winery Court
Templeton, CA 93465
T 805.434.2541
www.wildhorsewinery.com

Windward Vineyard
1380 Live Oak Road
Paso Robles, CA 93446
T 805.239.2565
www.windwardvineyard.com

York Mountain Winery
7505 York Mountain Road
Templeton, CA 93465
T 805.238.3925
www.yorkmountainwinery.com

Zenaida Cellars
1550 Highway 46 West
Paso Robles, CA 93446
T 805.227.0382
www.zenaidacellars.com

ARROYO GRANDE VALLEY / EDNA VALLEY

Alapay Cellars
491 First Street
P.O. Box 38
Avila Beach, CA 93424
T 805.595.2632
www.alapaycellars.com

Baileyana Winery
5828 Orcutt Road
San Luis Obispo, CA 93401
T 805.269.8200
www.baileyana.com

Cerro Caliente Cellars
831A Via Esteban
San Luis Obispo, CA 93401
T 805.544.2842
www.cerrocalientecellars.com

Claiborne & Churchill
2649 Carpenter Canyon Road
(Hwy 227)
San Luis Obispo, CA 93401
T 805.544.4066
www.claibornechurchill.com

Domaine Alfred
7525 Orcutt Road
San Luis Obispo, CA 93401
T 805.541.9463 (WINE)
www.domainealfred.com

Edna Valley Vineyard
2585 Biddle Ranch Road
San Luis Obispo, CA 93401
T 805.544.5855
www.ednavalley.com

Harrow Cellars
1800 Calle Joaquin
San Luis Obispo, CA 93405
T 805.544.1467
www.harrowcellars.com

Kelsey See Canyon Vineyards
1 Chardonnay
1947 See Canyon Road
San Luis Obispo, CA 93405
T 805.595.9700
www.kelseywine.com

Kynsi Winery
2212 Corbett Canyon Road
Arroyo Grande, CA 93420
T 805.544.8461
www.kynsi.com

Laetitia Vineyard and Winery
453 Laetitia Vineyard Drive
Arroyo Grande, CA 93420
T 888.809.VINE
www.laetitiawine.com

Rancho Arroyo Grande Winery & Vineyards
591 High Mountain Road
Arroyo Grande, CA 93420
T 805.474.0220 or 474.0385
www.ranchoarroyograndewines.com

River Wild Winery
591 High Mountain Road
Arroyo Grande, CA 93420
T 805.474.8299
www.riverwildwinery.com

Saucelito Canyon Vineyard
3080 Biddle Ranch Road
San Luis Obispo, CA 93401
T 805.543.2111
www.saucelitocanyon.com

Talley Vineyards
3031 Lopez Drive
Arroyo Grande, CA 93420
T 805.489.0446
www.talleyvineyards.com

Tolosa Winery
4910 Edna Road/Highway 277
San Luis Obispo, CA 93401
T 805.782.0500
www.tolosawinery.com

Wild Wood Vineyard & Winery
555 El Camino Real
San Luis Obispo, CA 93405
T 805.546.1088
www.wildwoodwine.com

Windermere/Cathy MacGregor Wines
3526 South Higuera, Ste. 240B
San Luis Obispo, CA 93401
T 805.542.0133
www.windmerewinery.com

Wolff Vineyards
6238 Orcutt Road
San Luis Obispo, CA 93401
T 805.781.0448
www.wolffvineyards.com

Index